THE BUSINESS
BEHIND BEAUTY

THE BUSINESS BEHIND BEAUTY

LAURA SERBAN

NEW DEGREE PRESS
COPYRIGHT © 2020 LAURA SERBAN
All rights reserved.

THE BUSINESS BEHIND BEAUTY

ISBN 978-1-64137-954-0 *Paperback*
      978-1-64137-771-3 *Kindle Ebook*
      978-1-64137-772-0 *Ebook*

CONTENTS

INTRODUCTION 7

PART I. LAYING THE FOUNDATION 15
CHAPTER 1. THE EVOLUTION OF THE BEAUTY INDUSTRY 17

PART II. EXAMINING THE VISIONARIES 29
CHAPTER 2. THE PRECEDENT OF INCLUSIVITY 31
CHAPTER 3. THE EXTRAORDINARY APPEAL
            OF THE ORDINARY 43
CHAPTER 4. ETHICAL ENTREPRENEURSHIP 55
CHAPTER 5. A FOUNDER-FIRST FRAMEWORK 69
CHAPTER 6. A FUSION OF HERITAGE WITH MODERNITY 79
CHAPTER 7. BEWARE THE BUBBLE OF INFLUENCER
            MARKETING 93
CHAPTER 8. MAKE EVERY PLATFORM MATTER 105
CHAPTER 9. THE AGE OF CLEAN BEAUTY 119
CHAPTER 10. SELL ME AN EXPERIENCE 131
CHAPTER 11. CLASS IS IN SESSION 147
CHAPTER 12. EMBRACING DIVERGENCE 159

PART III. ANTICIPATING THE FUTURE **171**
CHAPTER 13. THE DILEMMA OF INFLUENCER-CEOS   173
CHAPTER 14. CHALLENGES TO CONSUMERISM   187

CONCLUSION   199
REFERENCES   207
ACKNOWLEDGEMENTS   239

INTRODUCTION

"What does beauty mean to you?"

I asked this question to ten university students whom I interviewed in the fall of 2019. Their many insights are peppered throughout this book, but their answers to this initial question are what fascinated me most.

Each of the nine female students answered the question with definitions alluding to their sense of self. Some spoke of beauty as a reflection of happiness with who they are; others imagined beauty in terms of self-care and self-expression. One shared that she finds beauty in role models, another in emotions such as love, and another in nature. One commented on the cultural foundations of beauty standards throughout the world, while another emphasized the importance of uplifting marginalized women when speaking about beauty.

Notably, several of the female students claimed that they define beauty as kindness and authenticity.

The male student interpreted beauty through physical attributes, but he discussed a more emotional approach later in the interview. When I asked him if viewing beauty-related content on social media had ever changed his routine, he shared that some Instagram posts dedicated to taking care of dreadlocks inspired the confidence within him to start growing his own dreads.

Though it is challenging for most people to define what exactly beauty means, it is noteworthy that all ten students spoke of this quality in a deeply personal way that is linked to their sense of identity. When they pondered my question, they thought about themselves and how they are positioned in the world around them.

My interpretation of beauty falls under a similar umbrella. When I think of beauty, I think of community.

I have been watching cosmetics-related videos on YouTube for almost a decade, meaning that I'm an active member of the beauty community. Along with millions of people throughout the world, I consume content created by "beauty influencers" who review products, impart knowledge and techniques, and chat about their lives. Some of them amass such a substantial following that they collaborate on products with established companies or even launch their own ventures.

I revel in the rare moments in which I meet somebody who is also a part of this community. When we discuss the influencers who we support, the products that we love, and the scandals that rock the beauty world, it feels like we are connecting as old friends.

Beyond community, entrepreneurship also comes to mind when I think of beauty. Since I first clicked on a makeup tutorial at the beginning of high school, I have been exposed to boundless female entrepreneurship in the digital space. This appears both in the form of influencers, who are often able to make a living off of their social media presence, and in the form of indie companies.

Indie companies are startups that are unaffiliated with the main cosmetics conglomerates. These companies often resonate with Generation Z and Millennials in a very personal way by targeting the values that are most important to these customers. Some focus on environmental sustainability, ethical business practices, or using strictly non-irritable ingredients. Others emphasize inclusivity through extensive shade ranges for all complexions or through affordable prices. Some create a cult of personality around their founder, others rely very heavily on influencer endorsement, and many do both. A number of these companies have even achieved unicorn status, which means they are worth more than $1 billion.

Behind these indie ventures lie the entrepreneurs who nurtured them and rendered them relatable to young consumers.

What is especially striking to me is the fact that women launch many of these profitable indie beauty companies. I grew up with the understanding that entrepreneurship is a cornerstone of the American dream; however, this arena is de facto owned by white men. The percent of United States venture capital dollars that went to single female founders or all-female teams of founders hovered at around 2 percent annually from 2008 to 2018.[1] According to *Fortune*, "in 2018, all female founders put together received $10 billion less in funding than one e-cigarette company, Juul, took in by itself."[2]

Although men dominate the founder and CEO pool for large cosmetics conglomerates like L'Oréal, women have long been carving a place for themselves in the startup arena of this industry. From the days of Madam C.J. Walker, known as the first female self-made millionaire in the United States, beauty has been a space for female-led innovation, leadership, and ambition.

Walker was the first person in her family to be born free after the Thirteenth Amendment abolished slavery in 1865. Orphaned at seven years old and forced to contend with Jim Crow, Walker secured financial independence through beauty entrepreneurship.[3] In the words of the pioneer herself, "I am a woman who came from the cotton fields of the South. From there I got promoted to the washtub. From there I was promoted to the cook kitchen. And from there I promoted *myself* into the business of manufacturing hair goods and preparations."[4]

---

[1] Emma Hinchliffe, "Funding For Female Founders Stalled at 2.2 percent of VC Dollars in 2018," *Fortune*, January 28, 2019.

[2] Ibid.

[3] Henry Louis Gates, "Madam Walker, the First Black American Woman to Be a Self-Made Millionaire," PBS, accessed May 28, 2020.

[4] Barbara Thomas, "An American Pioneer Is Rediscovered," *Los Angeles Times*, February 15, 1999.

As a continuation of this legacy, this book focuses on how inspirational founders of today have promoted themselves into the cosmetics business. Their flourishing companies serve as proof that the world of beauty is an absolute hub of fast-paced entrepreneurship.

Despite many people's decision to demote it to the status of a frivolous hobby, the reality is that beauty is monumental. The global beauty industry has exploded in the past decade, becoming a $532 billion giant by the middle of 2019.[5] This growth is partly due to startups that expertly leverage social media's unprecedented access to millions. They tap into the core of the beauty community, captivating its new wave of young enthusiasts and challenging established conglomerates that have long dominated the industry.

Unfortunately, for an industry that has undergone such a fundamental transformation, it has not been comprehensively studied. This is troubling to me because I have personally witnessed its evolution and recognize the abundance of lessons to glean from studying its entrepreneurs. The ventures they started are products of a new kind of customer who envisions a different relationship with businesses than her parents did.

I argue that indie beauty companies are case studies for what Generation Z and Millennial consumers desire from a twenty-first-century business.

---

5   Bethany Biron, "Beauty Has Blown up to Be a $532 Billion Industry—and Analysts Say That These 4 Trends Will Make It Even Bigger," *Business Insider*, July 9, 2019.

These companies are typically founded by digital natives who have an innate understanding of how to employ each kind of social media to reach as broad an audience as possible. They understand how to foster their own communities of fans while simultaneously relating to the beauty community at large, and they know what kinds of products and brands are missing from the market. In short, they know how to honor our values and make themselves irresistible to us.

By analyzing both practical business strategies and the emotional desires of young people, this book, in many ways, transcends the beauty industry itself. I am therefore targeting a wide scope of readers.

I am speaking to consumers who want to hear the behind-the-scenes stories and motivations of inspirational founders.

I am speaking to entrepreneurs who desire to learn lessons from successful startups that are navigating uncharted territory.

I am speaking to marketers who need advice on how to create the kind of reciprocal relationship that young consumers seek.

I am speaking to corporate executives who want an insider's perspective of what is important to Generation Z and Millennials.

I am speaking to everybody who is curious about the joint effort between two generations to revolutionize a behemoth industry.

Let me introduce you to the business behind beauty in the twenty-first century.

PART I

LAYING THE FOUNDATION

CHAPTER 1

THE EVOLUTION OF THE BEAUTY INDUSTRY

———

One hundred sixty-nine billion.

That is the number of views that beauty-related content on YouTube generated in 2018 alone. Two years prior, when the boom of YouTube cosmetics videos began in earnest, the amount was fifty-nine billion. In 2010, it was a mere five billion.[6]

Before the 2010s, women who sought beauty products were typically constrained in both options and knowledge. Consumers were left to their own devices at drugstore retailers, or they depended on makeup counter employees at department stores to explain the function of products and the techniques needed to use them. Women were usually loyal to a small number of beauty companies, especially when they ventured into the luxury category.

---

6 J. Clement, "YouTube: Annual Beauty Content Views 2018," Statista, December 4, 2019.

With the invention of YouTube in 2005, beauty enthusiasts no longer had to rely on company employees, books, or magazines to learn how to paint their faces. YouTube ushered in an Information Age of the beauty industry, creating a beauty *community* that has become the bedrock of the beauty *industry*.

This community is spearheaded by beauty influencers who assume the role of a caring older sibling, best friend, or mentor. Early influencers like Michelle Phan, Marlena Stell, Jackie Aina, Patrick Starrr, Tati Westbrook, and NikkieTutorials created blueprints for teaching beauty techniques while simultaneously fostering a sense of friendship with their subscribers.

When influencers sit in front of their cameras and record videos for millions of young fans, they share not only product recommendations but also the private details of their lives. Their audiences, predominantly comprised of Generation Z and Millennials, become deeply devoted to hearing their perspectives, sharing their experiences, and vicariously living through their videos.

Certainly, the link between influencers and viewers is an example of a parasocial relationship, a one-sided relationship in which one person invests emotions while the other is unaware of the first's existence.[7] This kind of connection is typically associated with celebrities and their fans. However, influencers are unlike celebrities in one vital way: they

---

7   Nomi-Kaie Bennett, Amy Rossmeisl, Karisma Turner, Billy Holcombe, Robin Young, Tiffany Brown, and Heather Key, "Parasocial Relationships: The Nature of Celebrity Fascinations," Find a Psychologist, accessed May 28, 2020.

routinely share intimate parts of their lives with their audiences. Their public personas are usually not polished and controlled by publicists, and as a result, viewers see their raw and unfiltered emotions.

Few other industries have had such extensive and influential communities built around them. In fact, the beauty community is omnipresent for many young people. The influencers we follow and support on these platforms permeate our daily lives. From sunup to sundown, their content is free and easily accessible. They cheer us up, share products with us, teach us makeup skills, and provide a haven from the world around us. They inspire us to be creative and confident. They amuse us with their publicized personal lives, which often provide the fodder for scandals that fascinate the internet. They remind us that we are not alone.

The creation of Instagram in 2010 further expanded this capacity to connect and share knowledge with millions of other beauty enthusiasts.

As YouTube influencer Jaclyn Hill declared in an interview with *Refinery29*, "In the past, we had the greats like Kevyn Aucoin. They wrote books, and you went to Barnes & Noble and you got the books and that was it—you had your fifty pages, and you're done. Now you have these artists that are doing celebrities and runway and Fashion Week—the top people in the world—[and they're] right there on Instagram."[8]

---

8   Mi-Anne Chan, "Get Ready: Jaclyn Hill's New Becca Products Are Even Better Than Her Last," *Refinery29*, May 20, 2016.

Artists were not the only ones who took advantage of the platform. Led by an entrepreneurial spirit, indie companies that are independent of large conglomerates began to spring up and achieve cult followings on Instagram without spending money on traditional advertising. The platform provided a new sales channel, enabling companies to treat their feed like a virtual store in which they showcase each product and how to use it. Rather than invest in brick-and-mortar stores, indie companies embrace e-commerce and social media to directly connect with Generation Z and Millennials.

Now, the consumer is the expert and makes her own informed choices from a marketplace of seemingly endless options.

According to Tarang Amin, CEO of e.l.f. Beauty, "The internet has become the true equalizer." His company was founded online in 2014 with the mission of offering affordable cosmetics that perform to the standard of professional grade products. Its success stems in part from consumers' increased willingness to shop across segments. "They are just as likely to have a Chanel item as an e.l.f item," Tarang asserted in *The Wall Street Journal*.[9]

Even brick-and-mortar retailers like Sephora and Ulta Beauty are taking advantage of this new age of consumers as the "experts." They put out testers for each product, allowing customers to feel the consistency of the formula and to see the color applied on their skin. Employees are available to provide guidance, but many customers have already read or

---

9   Sharon Terlep, "Aging Beauty Brands Want a Facelift," *The Wall Street Journal*, February 5, 2018.

watched online reviews of the products that they are interested in. They enter the store knowing exactly what to buy. After all, influencers are continuously evaluating each product that is being released.

The opinions of YouTube influencers carry significant weight among young viewers. Negative reviews that target poor product quality, lack of shade inclusivity in complexion ranges, and questionable actions of CEOs have destroyed the reputation of many beauty companies. Some influencers have decided to boycott certain companies altogether, and their subscribers have followed along. Even companies owned by influencers-turned-CEOs are not safe from the "cancel culture" that ignites mass boycotting.

Cancel culture is also spurred by "drama channels," or YouTube channels dedicated to reporting on scandals among influencers or between influencers and companies. Their investigative pieces influence public opinion and provide a platform for disgruntled consumers to voice their concerns. Many drama channels, much like influencers, serve as a sort of lever of accountability in the industry.

One instance of cancel culture was comically named Dramageddon, which is a reference to the Bible's Armageddon, the last battle between the forces of good and evil. Dramageddon began in 2018 as a squabble within a friend group of prominent influencers, but it deteriorated into depravity when Twitter users discovered old, racist tweets from some of the influencers. Laura Lee received the brunt of the "cancelling" when she posted an apology video that was incoherent and appeared disingenuous. She immediately lost more than half a million subscribers, and cosmetic companies that were working with her ended the relationship. Laura's YouTube channel, which was acquiring well over one hundred thousand new subscribers monthly before Dramageddon, has barely gained any since.[10]

On the other hand, the beauty community has a tremendous power to uplift people. One such example appears in the form of supporting companies founded by a person from a marginalized group. YouTuber Jackie Aina has created makeup tutorials in which she challenges herself to use only products from women-owned companies, black-owned companies, and Muslim-owned companies. Videos containing only products from Latina-owned companies are also popular. Posts similar to these exist across all platforms, and they serve as a means of spotlighting founders who are underrepresented in business.

When I interviewed Kiarie Mumbi, a biology major and pre-medicine student at Georgetown University, he shared the influence that this kind of advocacy has had on his own purchasing decisions: "I began to use hair products from a company named Jamaican Mango and Lime after seeing Instagram posts urging people to support black-owned businesses. I think that it is important to uplift founders who are creating wonderful products but who do not get the exposure that they deserve."

This is the atmosphere of beauty today.

---

10 "Laura Lee," Social Blade, accessed May 28, 2020.

The advent of social media has made it possible to directly access millions of consumers who are ready to throw their support behind people and companies that they believe in. Nonetheless, it can be difficult for some to navigate an arena in which all eyes are on them. The cases of influencers and companies who have been cancelled are evidence that what consumers give, they can easily take away.

Another consequence of the social media explosion is that the beauty industry has become oversaturated. New startups are constantly birthed, and existing companies are following the example of fast fashion by flooding the market with products. As a result of this crowded atmosphere, businesses are motivated to constantly discover creative ways to attract the attention of consumers and influencers alike. If one company fails to keep up, there are dozens of others who have their fingers squarely on the pulse.

In September 2019, *Forbes* reported that the global beauty industry was worth $532 billion and that it would continue to "advance at a 5 percent to 7 percent compound annual growth rate to reach or exceed $800 billion by 2025."[11] Much of that growth is due to indie beauty companies. As Credit Suisse analysts reported in 2018, "the global beauty market is fragmenting, with the top twenty [companies] steadily losing market share to startups."[12]

---

[11] Pamela Danziger, "6 Trends Shaping The Future Of The $532B Beauty Business," *Forbes*, September 1, 2019.

[12] Anthony Mirhaydari, "Beauty for All: How Deciem Is Disrupting the Skincare Industry," PitchBook, April 26, 2018.

Entrepreneurs have leveraged the capacity to connect with millions of people in order to launch indie companies. Since they are not affiliated with the few beauty giants such as Estée Lauder Companies, L'Oréal, and Shiseido, who have long dominated the industry, these indie founders can craft their own unique brands and engage directly with their fans.

In a crowded and globally connected marketplace, entrepreneurs are successfully attracting the attention of Generation Z and Millennials by redefining the consumer-brand relationship.

At their core, Generation Z and Millennials operate in a world of continuous streams of information and instant communication. They feel deeply connected to the world around them, and on topics such as climate change, diversity, beauty standards, and mental health, they are conceptualizing better alternatives to the status quo. Though young, they are already crafting a new world.

One of the critical ways in which Generation Z and Millennials indicate their desires is through their purchases. Members of these generations, more so than their parents or grandparents, want to support companies whose brand resonates personally with them.

Ashly Paulino, a Georgetown University English major whom I interviewed, perfectly encapsulated this phenomenon with the following statement: "My relationship to the beauty industry is that I'm not really ever invested in the product; I'm invested in the mission behind the company." She went on to assert that "the hallmark of Generation Z is to reclaim the power behind being a consumer. By choosing to either buy or not buy your products, we can make or break your company."

Many of the companies that I discuss in the book have become billion-dollar businesses because they understand this perspective. In response, they have created distinctive brand identities that incite the loyalty of young people by prioritizing inclusivity, ethics, authenticity, promotions by influencers, and much more. They understand that Generation Z and Millennials demand a kind of reciprocity from companies that did not exist in the past, and they cultivate it by integrating their consumers' input into their business model.

As a result, many indie companies have triumphed. According to research firm Kline & Co., "the rise of upstart [businesses] has come as traditional beauty companies that have long dominated the $52 billion US market have faltered. Independent makeup [companies'] sales grew 24 percent in 2017, compared with the market average of 5.9 percent."[13]

A perfect example is Anastasia Beverly Hills, an indie company that is one of the original beauty companies to harness the power of Instagram. *The Wall Street Journal* reported that the company "had a pretax profit of $180 million [in 2017]… In contrast, Revlon Inc., a more established [company], had a $133.5 million pretax profit. And revenue is growing at a

---

13   Jaewon Kang, "Celebrities Like Kylie Jenner Are Upending the $52 Billion Beauty Industry," *The Wall Street Journal*, November 28, 2018.

much faster pace for the younger rival, 64 percent from 2014 to 2017 versus 12 percent for Revlon."[14]

The old giants, which are generally not as adept at marketing to Generation Z and Millennials, have accepted the shifting trends of the industry. Instead of reinventing the wheel, they are acquiring highly lucrative indie companies that already possess young and loyal fanbases. The challenge is to maintain the branding that made these small companies so appealing in the first place.

On all fronts, beauty is radically evolving. Few other industries have been so drastically transformed in such a short time.

In part because the topic of beauty is deeply personal and in part because of tremendous competition, the beauty industry is highly attuned to what the emerging wave of customers desires for themselves and their society. Amid the Information Age of beauty, entrepreneurs are creating ventures that celebrate the new reality of consumers as experts in products and partners in business.

In short, there is a democratization occurring in beauty. Now, the industry is continuously invigorated with new visionaries who finally have the opportunity to inject their own innovative beliefs and ideas into a landscape governed by consumers.

The next section analyzes the business strategies of eleven cosmetics and skincare companies that were either born out

---

14   Ibid.

of this new beauty industry or that have skillfully adapted to it. All are quintessential twenty-first-century businesses that have captivated Generation Z and Millennials. The stories of these companies are tracked through their founders, who have each discovered their own means of building a venture that stands out from its competitors.

These eleven case studies serve as microcosms for the kinds of businesses that are thriving in the dynamic new world molded by Generation Z and Millennials.

PART II

EXAMINING THE VISIONARIES

CHAPTER 2

THE PRECEDENT OF INCLUSIVITY

In September 2017, a revolutionary force challenged the standards of the beauty industry and fundamentally altered the landscape of cosmetics. Social media blew up as the message spread first among makeup enthusiasts and then to broader Twitter, Instagram, and YouTube audiences: Fenty Beauty by Rihanna had launched in Sephora with forty foundation shades.

Fenty Beauty emerged onto a scene of pitiful inclusivity. While a few mainstream companies already featured a robust selection of dark foundation tones, dark-skinned customers faced limited options in the majority of foundation ranges. The deep-dark category, which is the darkest on the complexion spectrum, was especially ignored. Moreover, most of the companies that did already offer around forty shades, such as Maybelline, Make Up For Ever, MAC Cosmetics, and Lancôme, had not launched them all at once. With the exception of Make Up For Ever, the rest of them had gradually added to their ranges throughout the years.

When Fenty Beauty hit the shelves in this atmosphere of shade exclusivity, it garnered such pronounced approval that it dominated conversations about beauty for months. YouTube influencers who reviewed the initial launch received millions of views on their videos, customers flocked to Sephora in fear of the collection inevitably selling out, and students in high school and college complimented each other's incorporation of Fenty products into their makeup looks.

Though this was Rihanna's first cosmetics venture, the beauty community praised Fenty Beauty.

Its immediate success is evident: *Forbes* reported that the company racked up a reported $100 million in sales in the first few weeks of its initial launch in Sephora.[15] When *Vogue* posted a YouTube video called "Rihanna's Epic 10-Minute Guide to Going Out Makeup" eight months after Fenty Beauty's launch, the video obtained over thirty million views.[16] By mid-2019, the company was conservatively valued at more than $3 billion.[17]

---

15 Natalie Robehmed, "How Rihanna Created A $600 Million Fortune—And Became The World's Richest Female Musician," *Forbes*, June 4, 2019.

16 *Vogue*, "Rihanna's Epic 10-Minute Guide to Going Out Makeup | Beauty Secrets," May 3, 2018, video, 10:28.

17 Natalie Robehmed, "How Rihanna Created A $600 Million Fortune—And Became The World's Richest Female Musician," *Forbes*, June 4, 2019.

Clearly, Rihanna struck a chord. By fostering a mantra of authentic inclusivity through every aspect of its brand, Fenty Beauty deeply resonates with young consumers.

In a move that further solidified its intentions as genuine, the company released a marketing campaign that went viral on social media. People of diverse races and skin tones ranging from deep dark to very fair adorned the initial launch's promotional pictures and videos on Instagram, YouTube, and the Fenty website. The official launch video featured blips of women like Halima Aden, who wore a hijab, and Paloma Elsesser, a plus-size model.[18]

The visuals in this campaign set the tone for the marketing that Fenty Beauty continues to implement. One scroll through the company's social media platforms is enough to see that its motto, "Beauty for All," is always exemplified. As Fenty Project Manager Jennifer Rosales remarked, Rihanna is "not telling everyone to be like her. She's telling everyone, 'You can feel this good too. You just gotta do you.'"[19]

Furthermore, Rihanna emphasizes authentic inclusivity by intertwining her own values with the company's empowering message. Fenty Beauty is a partnership between Rihanna and Kendo, the incubator arm of the French Louis Vuitton Moër Hennessy (LVMH) conglomerate. As an incubator, Kendo helped to transform Rihanna's idea into an actual company. Since LVMH owns part of Fenty Beauty, it is not exactly an

---

[18] *Snobette*, "Rihanna Debuts Fenty Beauty Campaign Ft. Halima Aden, Slick Woods and Leomie Anderson," September 1, 2017, video, 1:14.

[19] Abby Aguirre, "Rihanna Talks Fenty, That Long-Awaited Album, and President Trump," *Vogue*, October 9, 2019.

indie venture. However, Fenty Beauty is anything but corporate. The company intentionally embodies the affable and confident spirit of Rihanna; Fenty is her last name after all. Rather than provide a generic celebrity endorsement, which would have appeared distant in the deeply personal context of the beauty community, she embraced the role of founder.

For example, in a thirty-minute YouTube video called "Artistry and Beauty Talk with Rihanna," which was recorded in July 2019 and has almost one million views, Rihanna stood in front of a crowd of fans and discussed each of her products. As makeup artists demonstrated how to apply them, she integrated elements from her personal life into the presentation. She recounted her earliest conception of beauty, which revolved around her dark-skinned mother. She also revealed her need for long-wearing matte foundations for lengthy red carpet events and performances, which explains the formulation of Fenty Beauty's first foundation.[20]

By sharing these details from her life, Rihanna humanized Fenty Beauty and reiterated that she is extremely hands-on in the creative process. Therefore, when she declared at the company's launch party, "I want women of all shades to feel included, and all races and all cultures to be a part of this," it felt authentic to the consumer that the company was a natural product of Rihanna's own inclusive vision of beauty.[21]

---

20 *Fenty Beauty by Rihanna*, "Artistry & Beauty Talk With Rihanna," July 7, 2019, video, 29:13.

21 *E! Red Carpet & Award Shows*, "Rihanna Talks New Fenty Beauty Line at NYFW," September 8, 2017, video, 2:06.

She has implemented this strategy in interviews as well, often sharing her inspiration behind Fenty Beauty's marketing. At the 2017 Diamond Ball, the annual black-tie fundraiser for Rihanna's nonprofit Clara Lionel Foundation, she declared "I have this perception that my friends are the consumer, and if it doesn't work on them, then I'm not doing it."[22]

Though Rihanna was a music-based celebrity and an outsider to the cosmetics industry when her company launched, she earned the beauty community's respect with her belief that nobody deserves to be a token or an afterthought. She funneled this message through Fenty Beauty, crafting a brainchild that is personal and authentic.

YouTube influencers were eager to support the revolution that she incited in beauty, and their reviews engendered mass enthusiasm.

One notable example is Nyma Tang, a Sudanese-American influencer who created a video series named *The Darkest Shade*, in which she tests the darkest version of makeup companies' products to see if they are complementary to her deep-dark skin. On the weekend of Fenty Beauty's launch, she wrote on Instagram, "I saw other dark-skinned girls in Sephora getting matched in this foundation, and it literally melted by heart."[23] When she subsequently tested the darkest

---

22 *AP Archive*, "Rihanna's Charity Diamond Ball Makes a 'Scary' Move to New York," September 19, 2017, video, 4:59.

23 Lindsay Schallon, Rachel Nussbaum, and Teryn Payne, "One Year Later, This Is the Real Effect Fenty Has Had on the Beauty Industry," *Glamour*, September 14, 2018.

hue on YouTube, which matched her complexion, the video garnered over eleven million views.[24]

Influencer Alissa Ashly also reviewed the initial launch in a video that has been watched more than one million times. She declared, "I just respect it a lot that they really put effort into a full shade range…and I use brands that I respect." Alissa also expressed her excitement for future Fenty Beauty launches, affirming, "I'm inspired because we have a new brand that we finally all stand for."[25]

Fenty Beauty was so positively received by the beauty community because it set a new precedent on three fronts.

Firstly, it emphasized the importance of not only creating products for everybody but also advertising them through models that reflect true diversity. One look at the current Fenty Beauty Instagram page is enough to see that diversity is still as much a part of its DNA as it was when the company initially launched.

Secondly, it demonstrated the importance of offering a wide enough selection in each shade category to account for varying undertones underneath the skin's surface. Each person's undertone falls into one of three categories: warm, cool, and neutral. Skin is "warm" if its underlying color is yellow or gold, "cool" if the underlying color is pink or red, and "neutral" if there is a mixture of warm and cool tones. Cognizant

---

24 *Nyma Tang*, "Fenty Beauty Pro Filt'r Foundation Review | #thedarkestshade," September 11, 2017, video, 10:15.

25 *Alissa Ashley*, "Fenty Beauty by Rihanna Review + Tutorial," September 11, 2017, video, 17:37.

of how these hues subtly affect complexions, Fenty Beauty created a spectrum that truly reflects the diversity of human skin.

This effort is especially important in the United States, which is undergoing a demographic shift. As Balanda Atis, the manager of L'Oréal's Multicultural Beauty Lab, declared, "a skin tone is born every day…The minority is now the majority. In order for us to keep up with demand, we have to be diverse."[26]

The third precedent set by Fenty Beauty arrived in the form of a challenge: Rihanna disputed the assumption that black women do not spend as much as their non-black counterparts on cosmetics. Before Fenty Beauty, most companies left their dark category bleakly underserved until they could review the popularity of their few initial dark shades. As influencer Jackie Aina stated in her YouTube video reviewing Fenty Beauty, which received over three million views, "White businesses get funded based on potential, and black businesses get funded based on proof."[27]

Fenty Beauty was Rihanna's courageous rebuttal to this status quo. Not only is it one of the only companies to ever invest in such an expansive complexion range all at once, but it trekked into completely uncharted territory by doing so for its very first launch. It did not seek proof from its black customers; instead, Rihanna assumed the risk of betting on absolute inclusion from the start.

---

[26] Jessica Cruel and Amber Rambharose, "'Nude' Is No Longer One Shade Fits All," *Glamour*, March 21, 2018.

[27] *Jackie Aina*, "Fenty Beauty?! Hot Or Hmmm," September 14, 2017, video, 23:46.

It was a breath of fresh air in a market that had long ignored calls for change. The company recognized the desire of all customers to be seen and understood, and it was in turn compensated with loyalty and excitement by the beauty community as a whole.

It even ignited a phenomenon named the "Fenty Effect," in which other companies attempted to catch up to Rihanna's example of inclusion. Dior, Covergirl, Cover FX, Revlon, NYX Professional Makeup, Estée Lauder, ColourPop, and others either expanded their collections or launched new ones with at least forty shades, which became the magic number.[28], [29] In one extreme measure, Pür Cosmetics launched a foundation in one hundred hues.

However, some companies appeared to be jumping on the bandwagon without the intentionality that Fenty Beauty possessed. Influencers stressed that expansive ranges are only useful if the shades have correct undertones; dark foundations with green or gray underlying pigments would likely not match anybody's complexion. They also emphasized that besides creating products for everybody, companies need to work with diverse models and influencers to indicate that inclusivity is not just a passing trend for them.

Alexandra Morris, a biology major and pre-medicine student at Georgetown University, honed in on the importance of genuine motives when I interviewed her: "There are some

---

28 Kristina Rodulfo, "For New Foundation Ranges, 'Fenty 40' Is the Magic Number," *Elle*, May 31, 2018.

29 Priya Rao, "The Fenty Effect: How Beauty Brands Are Responding to the New 40-Shade Foundation Standard," *Glossy*, July 17, 2018.

companies that are working hard to show that everybody deserves to feel beautiful. The problem is that other companies are using the diversity and body positivity movements just to sell things. They are pretending to care about sparking long-term positive change, but in the end, they will be inclusive only as long as it is popular."

The Fenty Effect also sparked a wave of criticism and boycotting directed toward businesses that are uninterested in even the pretense of embracing everybody. When Tarte Cosmetics and Beauty Blender each launched foundations in 2018 with dismal shade distributions in the dark and deep-dark categories, the YouTube beauty community collectively denounced the companies.

Jackie Aina stated in her video reviewing Tarte's release that the company "has to be the most whitewashed brand out there, just from their marketing, their Instagram…They don't do anything that makes people feel included…This foundation launch just reinforced that."[30]

Tarte subsequently stopped producing batches of the fifteen-shade product and launched a new version with fifty tones.[31] Meanwhile, Beauty Blender expanded its thirty-two shades, which were primarily in the medium category, to

---

30 *Jackie Aina*, "Black Girls React to Tarte Shape Tape Foundation," January 16, 2018, video, 25:28.

31 Thatiana Diaz, "Tarte Is Pulling Its Shape Tape Foundation & Starting Over After Backlash," *Refinery29*, February 4, 2019.

forty.[32] However, the two companies struggled to repair their tarnished reputations.

In a nutshell, Fenty Beauty threw a checkmate to the rest of the beauty industry.

Rihanna's message was so impactful that her company became a cultural icon. Among its many accolades, Fenty Beauty was recognized as one of *Time*'s 2017 Best Inventions of the Year, received *Allure*'s 2018 Best of Beauty Breakthrough award for changing the industry, and won the 2018 and 2019 Services to Diversity award given by Vogue Beauty Awards.[33] These recognitions reflect the affection felt within and outside of the beauty community toward the company.

Its subsequent launches of powder products, concealers, and contour sticks have continued to reinforce its reputation. The company even expanded its shade range to fifty hues in 2019 in order to represent more undertones.

Kaie Jarvis, a political science major at Howard University, reflected on the company's acclaimed status when I interviewed her about the industry. She explained, "Fenty Beauty is legendary. It's legendary not because it's a *black* company, but because it was just accepted as a company for *everybody*." She further elaborated on the Fenty Effect, stating that the phenomenon is forcing the industry to "move in the right direction. It's dragging its feet, but it's moving."

---

32   Alexa Tietjen, "Beautyblender's Concealer Launch Strategy? Keep Your Harshest Critics Close," *WWD*, February 5, 2020.
33   "Fenty Stats: Awards: Beauty," Fenty Stats, accessed May 28, 2020.

As Kaie's comments indicate, Rihanna's beauty venture captivated Generation Z and Millennials with its bold message. It not only fills a vital marketplace need, but it also resonates with people's deep desire to belong. Rihanna's personal beliefs, channeled through her company, make people feel profoundly seen and accepted.

Fenty Beauty is the epitome of a celebrity-owned company that celebrates the consumer rather than the founder. Through a welcoming culture that rejects tokenization and pandering, it set the standard for successful brand differentiation through a strategy of authentic inclusivity.

CHAPTER 3

THE EXTRAORDINARY APPEAL OF THE ORDINARY

Two women stepped out of the Deciem storefront in London's Covent Garden. Their translucent shopping bags were stamped with the words "The Abnormal Beauty Company" in bold, black font. Immediately as they exited into the street, a security guard ushered in a pair of relieved customers who replaced the two women in the congested store. Behind them, a long line of people offered the guard a communal sigh of frustration as they braced themselves against the November wind and waited for more shoppers to exit.

Once inside the store, customers bustled past the industrial racks that held some of Deciem's lesser-known brands. Their attention was on the nook reserved for the company's shining star: The Ordinary.

Stacks of The Ordinary's products perched on floating shelves under descriptions like "Vitamins and Retinoids," "Direct Acids," and "More Molecules and Antioxidants." The labels on the shelves' glass dropper bottles were just as scientific in name: among them were AHA 30% + BHA 2% Peeling Solution, Niacinamide 10% + Zinc 1%, and Ascorbic Acid 8% + Alpha Arbutin 2%.

A strange phenomenon was occurring in this store: customers were deciphering the scientific jargon around them. Moving in a blur, they pushed past each other to test the consistency of formulas on their hands and drop bottles into their shopping carts. They knew the purpose of Vitamin C derivatives, where lactic acid belongs in a skincare regimen, and what items would cause irritation when used together. Some occasionally consulted the store employees or conducted their own research on their phones, but many confidently tossed oils, peptides, and Vitamin A, B, and C derivatives into their carts without a moment's hesitation.

How could this brand command such intrigue among young consumers despite the fact that its shopping experience mimicked a chemistry exam?

At the core of The Ordinary's success is its utter transparency.

It all began when its founder, an Iranian-Canadian computer scientist named Brandon Trauxe, began to work on software for a cosmetics laboratory. While scanning through data to monitor regulatory and compliance problems, Brandon noticed that one company's $1,000 cream cost just $2 to produce. He began to uncover the full extent of markups in skincare, realizing that businesses were selling false dreams meant to justify their products' inflated price tags.[34]

Brandon rejected this tactic, launching The Ordinary in 2016 with a focus on making skincare accessible through prices that better reflect the cost of production. The brand is one of many that are under the Deciem umbrella, and it has proved to be the most successful of them all. Despite being formulated with potent active ingredients, almost all of its skincare products are priced under $10.

For example, some of the brand's top items are the chemical exfoliants lactic acid and glycolic acid. The Ordinary sells a 5 percent lactic acid in a 30mL bottle for $6.50, with a stronger 10 percent version available for $6.80. It also offers a 7 percent glycolic acid in a 240mL bottle for $8.70.

These prices are astounding when compared to The Ordinary's top competitors: Sunday Riley's 30mL bottle of 5 percent lactic acid is $85 and Drunk Elephant's 50mL bottle of a 25 percent blend of acids is $80. A popular drugstore option is Pixie's 250mL bottle of 5 percent glycolic acid, which is sold for $29.

It may be true that The Ordinary's formulations are not as chemically elegant or complex as those from more expensive companies, which add ingredients that improve product texture and reduce irritability. However, the brand pleases millions of customers and has become a bestseller at Sephora and Ulta Beauty. Moreover, The Ordinary has countless positive

---

34   Kari Molvar, "Brandon Truaxe of Deciem," *Nuvo*, May 30, 2017.

reviews across YouTube by dermatologists and consumers alike, and it is usually listed in articles that discuss the best skincare products to try.

Much of its acclaim stems from its pricing, which permits people to experiment with different products and test what works for their skin. Dermatologist Davin Lim emphasized the importance of this in his YouTube video, "Dermatologist Review on The Ordinary," which has amassed more than 1.5 million views. While giving an overview of the brand, he claimed, "Here's the summary: you must be an idiot if you don't try it because it is unbelievable for what it's worth… with The Ordinary you cannot go wrong because skincare is as individual as you are."[35] As Davin suggests, the brand allows for the creation of a complete and individualized regimen for a fraction of the cost of a single product from another company.

Furthermore, The Ordinary employs a strategy of transparent marketing that minimizes costs while resonating with a new wave of consumers.

To analyze The Ordinary's marketing, it is critical to understand the skincare context of Generation Z and Millennial consumers. The Information Age of beauty, spurred by YouTube, nurtured a skincare community that provides easily accessible education. Influencers like Michelle Phan incorporated skincare videos into their channels from the early days of the platform. As time went on, professional

---

35 *Dr. Davin Lim*, "Skin Care | Dermatologist Review on The Ordinary," October 14, 2018, video, 13:06.

skincare-focused channels like Mixed Makeup and Beauty Within emerged, gaining millions of subscribers by trying out products, providing recommendations, and inviting dermatologists to speak to their audiences.

Some dermatologists, like Dr. Davin Lim and Dr. Dray, have created their own channels and attract millions of viewers with their professional perspectives. When I interviewed Natalie Wong, a wildlife conservation major at the University of Delaware, she affirmed that these doctors are generally the most reliable sources of information on social media "because they are knowledgeable and unbiased. Dr. Davin Lim's review provides legitimacy to The Ordinary and contributes to the idea that the brand relies on a bedrock of science rather than false advertising."

In addition to the explosion of information on YouTube, the exportation of Korean beauty products and regimens, collectively known as K-Beauty, also began to influence the American skincare market. Articles appeared about the Korean ten-step routine featuring two cleansers, an exfoliant, a toner, an essence, a serum, a mask, a moisturizer, an eye cream, and a morning sunscreen.[36] By 2016, Sephora and Ulta Beauty were selling hundreds of K-Beauty products, exposing American consumers to a new conception of skincare's potential.[37]

According to Theresa Yee, senior beauty editor of trend forecasting company WGSN, "There is a powerful community

---

36 Kelly Im, "How to 10-Step Your Skincare Regimen like a Korean," *Vogue*, January 10, 2018.
37 Rina Raphael, "Retailers Big And Small Want A Piece Of The Thriving Korean Beauty Business," *Fast Company*, September 23, 2016.

of 'skintelligent' consumers who are not only skincare savvy and highly informed about products and ingredients, but are shaping the market…they are super inquisitive and will investigate, research, and educate themselves on the ingredients before they make a purchasing decision."[38]

The Ordinary's mission of honest marketing fit perfectly into this atmosphere of boundless information and widespread curiosity about skincare.

The most evident example lies in The Ordinary's packaging, which lacks extreme claims and promises. Instead, the products come in white boxes with their scientific names written below the brand's tagline, "Clinical Formulations with Integrity." Inside, the formulas are housed in unadorned glass dropper bottles that look like lab prototypes, and most contain either a single active ingredient or a blend of just a few active ingredients.

The Ordinary's website follows the same honest, scientific approach. Each product description contains formula details, the intended purpose of use, and warnings about sun exposure and irritability. Some have extremely specific information like justifications for certain pH levels and updates about improvements in formula technologies, which particularly attracts "skintelligent" consumers. For the average person who is confused by the industry jargon, the skincare community on YouTube is an ideal place to learn how to start speaking the language of skincare.

---

38   Tanisha Pina, "The Skin-Care Industry Is Thriving—but How Long Can This Boom Last," Fashionista, January 24, 2019.

This reputation of integrity is also a priority in-store, as evidenced by Brandon's decision to give neither a commission nor a target for sales to store employees.[39] His ultimate goal was to make customers feel that they can trust the employees to look out for their best interests.

In terms of direct advertising, The Ordinary has relied on word-of-mouth promotion from its inception. Its cult following and positive online reviews have eliminated the need to ever spend significant amounts of money on marketing. When scrolling through Deciem's Instagram account, which is The Ordinary's primary advertising channel, there is a conspicuous lack of supermodels, celebrities, and influencers endorsing the products. Like the rest of The Ordinary's brand, the account relies on a simple yet high-impact aesthetic in which the focus of each post is always on the product and its realistic potential.

Even Brandon's own interviews are a lesson in how honesty can pay off.

In a YouTube video called "Busting Beauty B.S. With Deciem's Brandon Truaxe," which has been watched more than 150 thousand times, Brandon revealed exactly how The Ordinary is profitable. Its cost of production is very low because the formulas are made at an in-house lab and contain easily available chemicals in their most isolated forms; for instance, one of The Ordinary's Vitamin C products requires only twenty or thirty cents to make. Unlike its competitors,

---

39 *Nadine Baggott*, "Busting Beauty BS With Deciem's Brandon Truaxe," January 7, 2018, video, 30:32.

which allocate a high percentage of their budget to marketing, The Ordinary chooses to forego paid endorsements. It thereby achieves the approximate 10 percent profit margin standard that expensive skincare companies do, all while preserving its integrity in the eyes of consumers.[40]

In another interview with *Evening Standard*, Brandon denounced the industry tactic of selling expensive products through exaggerated claims. He shared his reason for subverting the norm, asserting, "In the computer world, everything is zero or one; something is either there or it isn't. I took an approach of saying 'Look, I can breathe some geekiness into it. Things either work or they don't.'"[41] Brandon's unique perspective set him up to peel back the façade of the industry and make affordable skincare that works. His brand does not need to depend on convincing ploys; rather, its results speak for themselves.

This firm belief in candor cultivated a perception of The Ordinary as a reputable powerhouse of active ingredients that prioritizes customers over profit. As word spread throughout social media of this innovative brand, young consumers began to flock to the website. Co-CEO Nicola Kilner explained in an interview with *Allure* that The Ordinary caused Deciem's business to quadruple in a year. After selling two million units total between 2013 and 2016, the company

---

40 Ibid.
41 Laura Craik, "Brandon Truaxe: the Man Who Will Change the Way You Buy Beauty," *Evening Standard*, May 4, 2017.

sold eight million just in 2017.[42] Due to The Ordinary, Deciem landed in the ranks of one-stop-shop skincare companies.

In fact, the sudden frenzy was too much to handle. When the brand later launched its $6.90 foundation, the waiting list was seventy-five thousand people strong.[43] Disgruntled customers took to Instagram to voice their complaints about the brand's inability to keep up with demand. Brandon later lamented that "it was the biggest disaster…We don't plan a waiting list. Nobody plans a waiting list. This is not an Hermès bag. It's skincare."[44]

In the midst of the chaos, Estée Lauder swooped in to offer a minority investment of $50 million that enabled The Ordinary to scale up.[45] It was a no-brainer for both parties: Estée Lauder wanted to invest in a skincare brand that would attract Generation Z and Millennials, and The Ordinary needed to rapidly grow its capacities.[46]

Within the next few months, Deciem rose to the challenge of meeting demand for The Ordinary's products. By December 2017, The Ordinary was introduced to Sephora's online store

---

42 Baze Mpinja, "Meet Deciem, the Industry-Changing Company Behind The Ordinary Skincare," *Allure*, December 28, 2017.

43 Daniela Morosini, "Everything You Need To Know About The World's Most Disruptive Beauty Brand," *Refinery29*, July 30, 2017.

44 Rachel Syme, "The Cult Skin-Care Brand Whose Secret Ingredient Is Being Dirt Cheap," *The New Yorker*, January 30, 2018.

45 Joseph Brean, "The Inside Story of How Deciem, the Abnormal Beauty Company, Lived up to Its Name," *Financial Post*, November 30, 2018.

46 Trefis Team, "Why Estee Lauder Invested In Multi-Brand Skincare Brand Deciem," *Forbes*, June 16, 2017.

and sold out entirely within a week.[47] Its products even circulated among celebrities; Kim Kardashian shared on her app that she uses The Ordinary's Granactive Retinoid 2% Emulsion, which is $9.80, in her regimen.[48]

While the revolutionary idea of affordable yet potent skincare took off, the visionary behind it began to change. In January 2018, Brandon announced on Deciem's Instagram that he would be controlling all marketing. What ensued was a prolonged period of bizarre behavior allegedly caused by drug abuse and mental health issues: Brandon fired Nicola and the entire United States team, began posting dead animals on Deciem's Instagram to rally against animal testing, accused his staff and investors of financial crimes, temporarily closed most of Deciem's stores, and asked his followers to call 911 because he needed help. Finally, in January 2019, Brandon fell to his death from his apartment block.[49][50]

Brandon's death is especially disheartening for those who realize the depth of change that he ignited within the skincare industry. He explained the appeal of his integrity-based approach in an interview with *Cosmetics Business*: "We are doing very normal things as humans, but in the corporate world, and especially in beauty, what we do seems to be

---

47 Rachel Syme, "The Cult Skin-Care Brand Whose Secret Ingredient Is Being Dirt Cheap," *The New Yorker*, January 30, 2018.

48 Macaela Mackenzie, "Kim Kardashian West Reveals Her Skin-Care Routine, Including The Ordinary's Retinoid Serum," *Allure*, January 26, 2018.

49 Jonah Engel Bromwich, "He Built, Then Nearly Broke, a Successful Beauty Start-Up. Can It Go on Without Him," *The New York Times*, April 17, 2019.

50 Anthony Mirhaydari, "Beauty for All: How Deciem Is Disrupting the Skincare Industry," PitchBook, April 26, 2018.

against the norm. Business is made up of people, and people are humans. When you take humanity out of a business—which is the norm in the world—no matter how much success, there is much less fun, much less authenticity."[51]

The Ordinary's respected reputation has enabled it to weather Brandon's personal struggles relatively well. In August 2019, the brand rolled out into Ulta Beauty's stores and website, further institutionalizing the Deciem phenomenon with Nicola at the helm.[52] According to the *New York Times*, Deciem was projected to sell more than $300 million of products in 2019.[53]

Despite its setbacks, the company is extraordinary in its honesty and accessibility. Brandon created a venture that completely disrupted the status quo, offering an alternative to drugstore products that were not very potent and luxury products that catered to the elite. He launched the first affordable brand to gain mass recognition for its extensive range of active ingredients, and his commitment to sincere marketing further captivated skin enthusiasts.

In the words of Nils Johnson, the co-founder of retailer Beautylish, Brandon was "more Silicon Valley than beauty."[54] Through the Ordinary, Brandon lifted the veil off of a

---

51 "How to Launch a Fast-Growing Cosmetics Company," Cosmetics Business, June 17, 2016.
52 "The Ordinary Launches At Ulta Beauty," Beauty Packaging, May 28, 2019.
53 Jonah Engel Bromwich, "He Built, Then Nearly Broke, a Successful Beauty Start-Up. Can It Go on Without Him," *The New York Times*, April 17, 2019.
54 Ibid.

secretive industry and enabled young consumers to put the knowledge that they accrued online into practice.

CHAPTER 4

ETHICAL ENTREPRENEURSHIP

A sharp, distinctive smell of layered essential oils wafted down the block in front of a London storefront. People bustled up and down the street, their noses turning toward the open door. As they paused to inhale the scent of hundreds of bath products, their eyes lingered on something strange in the store's window.

"Police have crossed the line."

Fake blue and white police tape emblazoned with this slogan was tacked onto Lush Cosmetics's United Kingdom storefronts in June 2018. Next to the tape was a picture of a man whose face was split between a police officer on one side and a civilian on the other. Across his chest were the capitalized, bold words, "PAID TO LIE."[55]

---

55 Martin Belam, "Cosmetics Retailer Lush Criticised by Police over 'Spycops' Ad Campaign," *The Guardian*, June 1, 2018.

This was Lush's latest campaign, which highlighted the scandal of spycops. These undercover police officers were a part of the British Metropolitan Police's Special Demonstration Squad, which operated between 1968 and 2011 to infiltrate British political organizations including the Labour Party, Green Party, and Socialist Party.[56],[57] In 2011, *The Guardian* broke a story that some spycops had entered into intimate relationships with members of leftist groups while the activists were unaware of their partners' status as undercover police officers. Some had even fathered children in these fake relationships, eventually disappearing and leaving their new families behind when their missions ended.[58],[59]

Although Lush's campaign was directed at this undercover police group, many people believed that the company was attacking the entire police force. Even the Home Secretary, Sajid Javid, chimed in to demonstrate his disapproval with the tweet, "Never thought I would see a mainstream British retailer running a public advertising campaign against our hardworking police."[60]

---

56 Chloe Hall, "Everything You Need to Know About Lush's Crazy Controversial #Spycops Campaign," *Elle*, June 6, 2018.

57 "An Alliance of People Spied on by Britain's Political Secret Police," Campaign Opposing Police Surveillance, February 26, 2020.

58 Paul Lewis, Rob Evans, and Rowenna Davis, "Ex-Wife of Police Spy Tells How She Fell in Love and Had Children with Him," *The Guardian*, January 19, 2011.

59 Emine Saner, "How the Lush Founders Went from Bath Bombs to the Spy Cops Row," *The Guardian*, June 20, 2018.

60 Ibid.

Why would one of the world's largest cosmetics company, which earned £524.4 million in revenue in 2018 alone, entangle itself in such a sensitive issue?[61]

Simply put, Lush's very reputation has been built upon a foundation of advocating for people, animals, and the planet. As Mark Constantine, one of the co-founders, stated in *The Guardian*, "The question I get asked most often is: 'What do you want to do? Sell bath bombs or save the world?' I see no reason why I can't do both."[62]

To understand Lush's activism, one must first analyze its origins.

Lush was started in 1994 by seven people in a small shop in Poole, England.[63] Mo and Mark Constantine, a wife and husband pair who are two of the founders, own 63 percent of the business.[64]

Mark became homeless at sixteen years old, living in a tent in a woodland area while working to afford food and clothing.[65] He found employment at a hair salon as an apprentice hairdresser, which eventually inspired him to return to school for

---

61 "Lush Profile," Craft, accessed May 28, 2020.

62 Emine Saner, "How the Lush Founders Went from Bath Bombs to the Spy Cops Row," *The Guardian*, June 20, 2018.

63 Ibid.

64 "Mark and Mo Constantine Net Worth," TheRichest, accessed May 28, 2020.

65 Hannah Westwater, "Lush Founder Mark Constantine Shares His Own Experience of Homelessness," *The Big Issue*, December 20, 2018.

trichology, the study of the hair and scalp.[66] He then began to make hair products for The Body Shop, a beauty company that emphasized ethical sourcing of ingredients and refused to test on animals.[67]

Inspired by his past of homelessness and his experience of working for The Body Shop, Mark became an entrepreneur who valued advocacy and charity. When he, Mo, and the five others decided to launch Lush, they committed to building an ethical business.

The founders have aligned their company with a variety of causes over the decades. Lush ran campaigns against the Guantánamo Bay detention center, publicly opposed fracking, and paid the legal fees of environmental activists.[68] It also continuously donates 100 percent of the price of its Charity Pot body lotion to grassroots organizations specializing in human rights, animal protection, and environmental justice issues.

Core to the company's ethos is its Fair Trade and Community Trade initiatives, which aim to support the individual people who grow and harvest the ingredients used in cosmetic products. Lush accomplishes this by purchasing as many of its ingredients as possible directly from community projects in locations where the raw materials are sourced. In addition to

---

66   Milly Ahlquist, "A Herbal Heritage: The Story of Lush and Henna Hair Dye," Lush, accessed May 28, 2020.
67   Hannah Westwater, "Lush Founder Mark Constantine Shares His Own Experience of Homelessness," *The Big Issue*, December 20, 2018.
68   Emine Saner, "How the Lush Founders Went from Bath Bombs to the Spy Cops Row," *The Guardian*, June 20, 2018.

partnering with these local projects, the company prioritizes worker's rights, environmental safety, animal protection, and carbon emissions related to transport.[69]

Lush is also a champion of fauna. It is 100 percent vegetarian, has never tested its products on animals, and refuses to buy ingredients from suppliers who do test on animals.[70] Its annual Lush Prize, the largest prize fund in the "non-animal testing" sector, awards £250,000 to support initiatives and research to end or replace animal testing. Between 2012 and 2018, it gave £2.19 million to one hundred ten winners in twenty-eight countries.[71] Its stance against animal testing is even reflected in its line of accessories; an instantly identifiable Lush item is the "Fighting Animal Testing" tote bag.

Lush's dedication to these advocacy and activism initiatives has produced a lucrative brand that its supporters identify with.

According to the Boston Consulting Group (BSG), young people are seeking to support companies that reflect their morals, namely those that are kind to the planet. BSG asserts that these consumers operate by the "Reciprocity Principle," in which they open their wallets for brands who, in return, lend them "status currency" among their peers. Status currency is defined as the "status and values that consumers

---

69 "Our Ethical Buying Policy," Lush, accessed May 28, 2020.
70 "Animal Testing: Our Policy," Lush, accessed May 29, 2020.
71 "The Lush Prize," Lush, accessed May 28, 2020.

wish to project through their purchasing decisions and brand affiliations."[72]

For young consumers, it often exists in the form of environmental sustainability, ethics, and advocacy.

On the heels of a consumer survey, global market research firm Nielsen revealed in 2018 that "Millennials are twice as likely (75 percent vs. 34 percent) [as] Baby Boomers to say they are definitely or probably changing their habits to reduce their impact on the environment. They're also more willing to pay more for products that contain environmentally friendly or sustainable ingredients (90 percent vs. 61 percent)…or products that have social responsibility claims (80 percent vs. 48 percent)."[73]

Furthermore, *Bloomberg* argued in 2019 that Generation Z is not only interested in environmentally friendly products but that it also expects companies to take firm political stances. This is "a departure from the days when consumer companies went to great pains to avoid politics." *Bloomberg* cited one survey of Generation Z consumers that found that "40 percent [said] they'd pay more for a product if they knew the company was promoting gender equality issues

---

[72] Christine Barton, Lara Koslow, and Christine Beauchamp, "How Millennials Are Changing the Face of Marketing Forever," BCG, January 15, 2014.

[73] "Was 2018 the Year of the Influential Sustainable Consumer," Nielsen, December 17, 2018.

and 42 percent for racial justice initiatives."[74] This generational attitude may explain Nike's 2018 partnership with Colin Kaepernick, which bolstered the Black Lives Matter movement.

The idea of the Reciprocity Principle begins to make more sense when considering the world that Generation Z and Millennials inhabit. At their fingertips is unlimited information about how businesses are affecting people, animals, and the planet. In an instant, they can search for statistics about the gender wage gap or particular instances of racial discrimination. They can find pictures of children working in mica mines or animals being experimented on in cosmetic testing facilities.

When I interviewed Racquel Jones, a computer science major and pre-dental student at Rutgers University, she stressed the importance of fair trade practices: "I feel uncomfortable buying a product knowing somebody slaved over it…it's horrible to know that people are working in these miserable conditions so that you can feel beautiful." She also asserted that *all* industries should take responsibility for the injustices perpetuated in the process of bringing their products to market.

Environmental destruction is even more of a ubiquitous subject, alarming young people across the world. When I interviewed Madeline Moreno, an international politics major at Georgetown University, she spoke passionately about the

---

74 Craig Giammona, Carolina Wilson, and Sarah Ponczek, "Investors' Guide to Gen Z: Weed, Social Justice and Kylie Jenner," *Bloomberg*, April 5, 2019.

dread that many of us feel about the future of our planet: "Our generation is faced with this looming threat of climate change and the idea that the earth is becoming uninhabitable because so many of our habits are unsustainable. In response, there is a desire to be more eco-friendly."

In this kind of atmosphere, it is natural for people to want to project the message that they are doing their part to help the world. Many businesses have caught on to these desires, but Lush is the epitome of a company that is perfectly poised to check off all of the social responsibility boxes.

In fact, it was far ahead of the ethical trend. The company was birthed by a group of people who were quite radical for their time. In a podcast episode published on Lush's YouTube channel called "Business Should Evolve with Ethics," Mo explained that "in the 70s and 80s...'ethics' was not a word that was mentioned...no one really understood you could damage the planet, neither did they really understand you could improve it."[75] But by Lush's birth in 1994, its founders were envisioning a new approach to doing business.

In that way, Lush has been in the vanguard of ethical entrepreneurship for all of its life. This ethos is imbedded in its DNA and is organically projected into every aspect of its image.

For instance, one of the most visible aspects of the company's brand is its minimal packaging. This tradition began

---

75 *Lush*, "Business Should Evolve with Ethics—Mo Constantine," December 23, 2016, video, 31:30.

as a necessity due to limited funding at Lush's inception, but the founders decided to continue the effort to minimize waste as the company expanded.[76] Besides, the products have always sold themselves. Their sharp aromas, bright colors, intricate shapes, and textured surfaces beckon customers into storefronts. The kaleidoscopic explosions of bath bombs particularly lend themselves to pictures and videos on social media. A bonus for young customers beyond the aesthetic value is the allure of purchasing according to morals.

On the digital front, the company constantly shares data associated with its efforts. Its website is filled with an abundance of detailed articles about its latest campaigns and information about the environmental impact of its products. For example, one article explains that 35 percent of Lush's products are sold "naked," or without any packaging at all, whereas others are housed in black pots and bottles made of 100 percent post-consumer plastic. It advertises its collection program for these containers, which can be returned to Lush stores in batches of five in exchange for a free face mask. This program, which enables the plastic to be remolded into new containers, effectively closes Lush's recycling loop.[77]

The company also communicates its actions through more than five hundred YouTube videos, which enjoy a combined view count of over twenty million. One of its video series showcases the different ways in which Lush participates in the ethical trade of raw materials. These videos feature

---

76 Rhik Samadder, "Observer Ethical Awards 2014 Winners: Lush," *The Guardian*, June 11, 2014.
77 "10 Things You Should Know about Lush Packaging," Lush, accessed May 29, 2020.

interviews with experts and growers on the farms where the ingredients are sourced. For example, one Lush presenter traveled to Kenya to record how the aloe used in Charity Pot is extracted by Maasai women at the Laikipia Permaculture Centre.[78] Another went to Colombia to show how Lush's fair trade organic cocoa butter comes from farmers in the Peace Community of San José de Apartadó; this community's residents have lost government funding because of their nonviolent stand against the country's civil war.[79]

Beyond this easily accessible information that Lush publishes, the company also benefits from media debate and word-of-mouth publicity around its controversial activism. Many of its campaigns, such the one that protested spycops in the United Kingdom, stir up significant attention and further solidify Lush's reputation as a socially responsible business.

According to *The Guardian*, Mo and Mark viewed the aftermath of the spycops campaign positively. Despite the political backlash and the influx of thirty thousand one-star Facebook reviews from people who had never shopped at the store, the campaign was an excellent way to fortify Lush's brand as a politically conscious company. After all, "the issue was talked about endlessly on social media and in newspapers and TV, it drew a response from the home secretary, the film [about the campaign] on Lush's website got more than one million views, and many of the victims [of spycops] were happy."[80]

---

78 *Lush*, "Source To Skin | Charity Pot," March 29, 2019, video, 7:15.
79 *Lush*, "Lush Buying Presents: Cocoa Butter," August 28, 2012, video, 11:48.
80 Emine Saner, "How the Lush Founders Went from Bath Bombs to the Spy Cops Row," *The Guardian*, June 20, 2018.

Another instance of Lush's contentious activism is its seed funding of £20,000 to a group that became Extinction Rebellion. In April 2019, this global environmental movement blockaded London's busiest roads for days, resulting in fifty-five bus route cancellations that affected 500 thousand people. After almost seven hundred protestors were arrested, police were forced to stop detaining people because the city's available cells had filled to capacity.[81][82]

A month later, *The Times* asked Mark about Lush's contribution to Extinction Rebellion. He responded by claiming, "They didn't say to us, 'We're going to freeze all of London and cause chaos.' If they had, we probably wouldn't have funded them." He paused and smirked. "Actually, maybe we would [have]."[83]

Lush has established an expansive digital footprint through two prongs: bold activism and detailed information. A simple Google search of its ethics induces a flood of videos and articles that discuss its many campaigns and provide information about its ingredient sourcing, manufacturing, packaging, shipping, and selling practices. The company has also garnered mentions in countless articles and videos about ethical businesses that consumers should support.

---

[81] Jack Hardy, "Extinction Rebellion: Climate Protesters Dodge Arrest after Police Run out of Cells," *The Telegraph*, April 16, 2019.

[82] Matthew Taylor and Damien Gayle, "Battle of Waterloo Bridge: A Week of Extinction Rebellion Protests," *The Guardian*, April 20, 2019.

[83] Sam Chambers, "Interview: Lush Cosmetics Boss Mark Constantine," *The Times*, May 19, 2019.

Since Lush makes its "do-good" brand so apparent through its extensive online presence, consumers are bound to be naturally introduced to its philosophy of fusing morality with entrepreneurship.

When Mo appeared on the "Business Should Evolve with Ethics" podcast episode, she declared that Lush does not want to barrage customers with information about its ethos. "I think we go about it in a fairly gentle way: you can read about it here, or you can experience it there, or you can stumble on it just because you've bought the product."[84]

The company takes care to publicize its efforts without self-righteous lecturing. As Mark puts it, "When you have businesses dipping in the gutter, someone only has to be 'alright.' We're not a marvelously ethical business; we're alright."[85] In fact, he fantasizes about winning a "Most Ethical Company" award so that he could "stand up there and go: 'If we won, how shit are the rest of you?'"[86]

As consumer buying habits change to favor businesses with an ethical approach, Lush embodies the ideal company of the future. Although it was not born out of the beauty industry of Generation Z and Millennials, it certainly is well-adapted to it.

---

84 *Lush*, "Business Should Evolve with Ethics—Mo Constantine," December 23, 2016, video, 31:30.

85 Kate Walters, "Mark Constantine: Lush," Startups, accessed May 28, 2020.

86 Emine Saner, "How the Lush Founders Went from Bath Bombs to the Spy Cops Row," *The Guardian*, June 20, 2018.

A key business strategy that has permitted Lush to continue its tradition of advocacy and activism is the founders' insistence that company ownership remain private. As Mark stated at the 2017 Employee Ownership Association's annual conference, "The majority of Lush's current shareholders are not in favor of ownership passing to other corporations, venture capitalists, or into public stocks and shares…Sometimes companies have more to them than financial gain. Every now and then, some may have a dream, a spirit, something intangible which doesn't show in the balance sheets."[87]

Mark has expressed this sentiment in many other interviews, claiming that he wants to honor the responsibility that he feels toward customers who support the company for its ethics. He believes that if the founders begin to allow equity investment, Lush would be restricted in the social responsibility measures that it could take. Citing the examples of The Body Shop, Ben and Jerry's, and Innocent Drinks, Mark argues that nearly all ethical businesses eventually get sold to large corporations and betray their original missions. As he puts it, "If you're half-owned by Coca-Cola, you can't start running around saying 'Close Guantanamo Bay' like we did."[88]

Considering its popularity, the company does not need to sacrifice its private ownership. Lush was built from its inception to flourish among value-minded customers, and in the age of Generation Z and Millennials, it is thriving. Its

---

[87] "Lush Announces 10 percent Move to Employee Ownership at EOA Conference," Employee Ownership Association, November 27, 2017.

[88] Kate Walters, "Mark Constantine: Lush," Startups, accessed May 28, 2020.

consumers want to project their own morals through their purchases, and there is significant status currency in supporting a business that is kind to people, animals, and the planet.

Lush's popularity lies in its radical message that consumers do not necessarily have to choose between capitalism and integrity. With every purchase of a bath bomb, they vote with their wallets for a future of ethical entrepreneurship.

CHAPTER 5

A FOUNDER-FIRST FRAMEWORK

Kylie Jenner stares unflinchingly from the glossy cover of *Forbes*. Her hair is smoothed back into a bun, and she is wearing a sleek black blazer with angular shoulder pads. The Kylie Cosmetics products that propelled her to stardom adorn her face without overpowering her features. *Forbes*'s announcement rapidly circulates throughout social media: the twenty-year-old is set to become the world's youngest self-made billionaire.[89]

When Kylie achieved billionaire status in March 2019, almost all of her wealth derived from Kylie Cosmetics. Although her makeup company was a mere three years old, it was worth $900 million at the time.[90]

---

89   Natalie Robehmed, "How 20-Year-Old Kylie Jenner Built A $900 Million Fortune In Less Than 3 Years," *Forbes*, July 11, 2018.

90   Natalie Robehmed, "At 21, Kylie Jenner Becomes The Youngest Self-Made Billionaire Ever," *Forbes*, March 5, 2019.

Its remarkable success was apparent from inception. Kylie's mother, Kris Jenner, divulged to *Women's Wear Daily* (*WWD*) that in the first eighteen months, Kylie Cosmetics had achieved an astounding $420 million in retail sale. *WWD* wrote, "For perspective,...Estée Lauder['s] Tom Ford Beauty was said to have reached revenues of $500 million after a decade, and the brand is considered to be one of the two fastest growing in Lauder's portfolio...L'Oréal's Lancôme finally [hit] the [billion-dollar] milestone in 2015 after eighty years."[91] By comparison, Kylie's explosion was exceptional.

Unlike Rihanna's Fenty Beauty, Kylie Cosmetics was created to directly reflect its founder. It is branded not as a company for everybody, but as a company for people who want to look like Kylie. Starting from the very first launch and with each subsequent one, the business has conflated Kylie's image with her makeup products. Therefore, the triumph of Kylie Cosmetics can only be understood by analyzing what makes Kylie so captivating to her Generation Z and Millennial fans.

At the core of her appeal is her capacity to combine celebrity status with personal connection. Kylie is a hybrid celebrity-influencer: she is simultaneously more engaging than true celebrities and more private than true influencers. This intriguing balance of aloofness and relatability has positioned her as a cultural icon.

Kylie's entrance into the public eye started at nine years old when she began to star in her family's *Keeping Up With the*

---

[91] Rachel Strugatz, "Kylie Jenner's Kylie Cosmetics On Way to Becoming $1B Brand," *WWD*, August 9, 2017.

Kardashians reality television show.[92] As her sister, Kim Kardashian, boosted the Kardashian-Jenner clan to fame, Kylie matured in front of flashing lights and rolling cameras. She became a household name in her own right at seventeen years old when she left teenagers transfixed by her sudden altered appearance.[93] With a few injections of the filler Juvéderm into her lips to achieve a plumper look, her journey to the cover of *Forbes* began in earnest.

As Kylie's abrupt transformation ignited the country's curiosity, she publicly claimed that her enhancement was the product of makeup and not of plastic surgery.[94] The YouTube beauty community responded in 2014 and 2015 with an outpour of tutorials speculating what nude lip pencil and lipstick combination Kylie was using from Mac Cosmetics to modify her features. Beauty influencers taught millions of their young subscribers how to meticulously overline and shade their lips to achieve the Kylie look.

In a YouTube video called "Let's Talk About Celebrity Beauty Brands," Amanda Elimian recounted those many months of hysteria: "Kylie single-handedly increased MAC's profits [probably] tenfold…She would wear a lipstick out [in public and] within hours, somebody would find what shade it was, despite [neither] Kylie nor her makeup artist saying anything…and it would sell out in literal milliseconds." One lip

---

[92] Amy Chozick, "Keeping Up With the Kardashian Cash Flow," *The New York Times*, March 30, 2019.

[93] Kayleen Schaefer, "Kylie Jenner Built a Business Empire out of Lip Kits and Fan Worship," *Vanity Fair*, October 21, 2016.

[94] Frank Lovece, "Kylie Jenner: Plastic Surgery Rumors 'Insulting,'" *Newsday*, April 10, 2014.

pencil that Kylie often wore was called Cork, and as Amanda remembers, it sold out nationwide and "was on backorder… for weeks, probably months."[95]

Meanwhile, Kylie constantly posted on Instagram and Snapchat, sharing her makeup looks without addressing the rumors. As her lips continued to expand, the fascination took a turn for the worse. In April 2015, the "Kylie Jenner Lip Challenge" spread like wildfire throughout the internet. This viral fad, in which teenagers sucked the air out of a shot glass until their lips temporarily swelled, alarmed parents and medical professionals.[96] Finally, on a May 2015 episode of *Keeping Up With the Kardashians*, Kylie confessed, "I have temporary lip fillers. It's just an insecurity of mine, and it's what I wanted to do."[97]

Despite this admission, teenagers remained engrossed with the youngest Kardashian; after all, she was using social media daily to evolve before their very eyes from one of Kim's many sisters into an instantly recognizable personality.

Capitalizing off of the internet's fascination, Kylie went to work developing lip products that would mimic the nude colors that she had become known for. She teased the launch of three lip kits, which comprised of a lip liner and a liquid

---

95 *Amandabb*, "Let's Talk About Celebrity Beauty Brands," February 6, 2020, video, 34:15.

96 Molly Mulshine, "Teenagers on Instagram Are Destroying Their Lips with Shot Glasses in an Attempt to Look like Kylie Jenner," *Business Insider*, April 21, 2015.

97 Kayleen Schaefer, "Kylie Jenner Built a Business Empire out of Lip Kits and Fan Worship," *Vanity Fair*, October 21, 2016.

matte lipstick in the same color, for months on Instagram. They sold out in seconds when they finally went on sale in November 2015.[98] By February 2016, she officially launched Kylie Cosmetics on Shopify, an e-commerce platform.[99]

Kylie continued to post regularly on her social media, advertising her products every time she turned on the camera and showed off her signature pout. Since her brand had always been focused on her makeup looks rather than intimate details of her life, it felt natural when she incorporated her own products into the barrage of daily posts.

Her persistent online presence contributed greatly to molding the current Instagram beauty standard of large lips. She also sparked numerous accusations that she appropriates and profits off of a feature traditionally associated with black women. In 2015, fifteen-year-old actress Amandla Stenberg described the hypocrisy associated with this phenomenon in a tweet: "While white women are praised for altering their bodies, plumping their lips and tanning their skin, black women are shamed although the same features exist on them naturally."[100] Given that this time period coincided with the rise of Black Lives Matter and national debates about racism, Kylie's lips touched a nerve for many.

---

98 Natalie Robehmed, "How 20-Year-Old Kylie Jenner Built A $900 Million Fortune In Less Than 3 Years," *Forbes*, July 11, 2018.

99 Ibid.

100 Brianna Arps, "I Used to Get Bullied for Having Naturally Full Lips—but Now That I Love Them, People Accuse Me of Copying Kylie Jenner," *Insider*, July 21, 2017.

Despite these concerns, young fans continued to flock to her account, resonating with Kylie's transition from an awkward and insecure teenager into an Instagram icon of desirability. On her end, Kylie rode the obsessive wave of Juvéderm-ed lips among white girls and women, implicitly suggesting with the launch of her lip kits that her makeup products can help consumers match her aesthetic. After all, she did claim for months that her lips were the product of makeup techniques. This suggestion, which was present from the beginning of Kylie Cosmetics, paved the way for the company's approach of fusing itself with its nationally recognizable founder.

Kylie Cosmetics's strategy of conflation is perfectly encapsulated in its products. Some of the most popular ones are part of limited edition assortments that celebrate Kylie and the people in her life. For example, the company always releases a yearly birthday collection in August, Kylie's birthday month. This tradition has expanded to include her daughter Stormi, who has her own annual birthday collection in February. Kylie has even invited her family and friends to collaborate on products; Kris, Kim, Khloe, Kourtney, and her former best friend Jordyn Woods have each created a collection with Kylie Cosmetics.

The message is clear: when her followers purchase these little pieces that reflect their idol's life, they can, by extension, become a little more like Kylie. Even her company's "About" page drives home this message by declaring, "Kylie has worked hard to create a line of products that she feels captures the Kylie Jenner aesthetic."[101]

---

[101] "About," Kylie Cosmetics, accessed May 29, 2020.

The fusion of Kylie with her business is also evident from the company's Instagram marketing. The Kylie Cosmetics official account typically features a picture of Kylie sporting her own products on a daily basis. In fact, the longest that the account goes without posting its founder is around three days. By comparison, Fenty Beauty's Instagram account very rarely posts images of Rihanna.

Kylie also advertises her makeup items on her personal Instagram account, which, at more than 180 million followers, easily trumps the company account's twenty-four million. She intersperses campaign shoots, launch information for new collections, and product images among her usual pictures of her outfits, family, friends, and trips.

The thread of conflation continues even into Kylie Cosmetics's pop-up stores. According to Kylie's Shopify profile, her pop-ups are meant to be a "living, breathing thing" that embody what the brand feels, sounds, and smells like. Kylie's first one was in Westfield Mall in Los Angeles and featured "a replica Kylie bedroom [and] selfie station." Shopify calls these events "the embodiment of Kylie Cosmetics—ultimately the embodiment of Kylie, the person."[102]

It is evident that in the case of Kylie Cosmetics, the founder and the venture cannot be divorced from each other. The business draws its very identity from Kylie, who enjoys a social media fanbase that amounts to half of the United States population. However, her strategy forces her to contend with a question that few other billionaires face: what

---

102 "The Kylie Cosmetics Story," Shopify, accessed May 29, 2020.

will be the future of a company that is immensely reliant on the popularity of a single individual?

Though Kylie Cosmetics has been incubated by umbrella company Seed Beauty from the beginning, Kylie has always been at the forefront of the venture. Seed Beauty, which also owns ColourPop and incubates Kim Kardashian's KKW Beauty, is known for strategic partnerships that rely on influencers' and celebrities' social media channels to drive sales. In exchange, Seed Beauty manages the details of product development, manufacturing, and order fulfillment. Its founders, siblings Laura and John Nelson, agreed that Kylie would own 100 percent of her company in exchange for a percentage of sales.[103]

But what happens if Kylie wants to move onto something else?

Loose Threads, a website that analyzes consumer companies, observed, "An acquirer can't buy Kylie's personal audience of hundreds of millions of people. Instead, they would have to settle for buying the Kylie Cosmetics social accounts, which have a fraction of the following…If Kylie sold her brand, she would spend much less time working on it, and the association between the brand and its founder would start to fade."[104]

And therein lies the weakness in a founder-first framework.

---

103 "Kylie Cosmetics and the Value Paradox of Celebrity Brands," Loose Threads, accessed May 29, 2020.

104 Ibid.

While Fenty Beauty, also a celebrity-led company, built its branding off of making everybody feel included in the brand's vision, Kylie Cosmetics took an alternative route. Kylie's business model is more personal to her; when consumers think of Kylie Cosmetics, they think of Kylie and not much else. As a result, she is locked into an inflexible situation in which the longevity of her company depends on her direct involvement. After all, it is *Kylie* the individual who sold her lips to Generation Z and Millennials.

This issue arose when she announced in November 2019 that conglomerate Coty Inc. would purchase a 51 percent stake in her beauty business for $600 million; the deal, which was finalized in January 2020, included Kylie Cosmetics and the much smaller Kylie Skin.[105] According to Coty's CFO, Pierre-André Terisse, half of Kylie's followers live outside of the United States while the vast majority of her sales are from within the country. As a beauty giant, Coty hopes to use its own global footprint to take full advantage of Kylie's international social media followers. For this plan to work, Kylie will remain the creative lead on product development and, most importantly, on marketing.[106]

Li Jin, a partner at venture capital firm Andreessen Horowitz, is doubtful that Kylie's founder-first approach is optimal in the long term. She recommends that the company's branding shift to a mission-oriented purpose, asserting, "She can align her brand with a broader shift in women's attitudes: today,

---

105 "Kylie Jenner," *Forbes*, accessed May 29, 2020.
106 Madeline Berg, "Billionaire Kylie Jenner To Cash In On Her Cosmetics Line With $600 Million Sale To Coty," *Forbes*, November 18, 2019.

that could be makeup as self-expression and a celebration of individuality and diversity."

For now, Kylie is continuing to serve as the face of an empire built upon her own following. Her unique role as a hybrid celebrity-influencer has attracted hundreds of millions of fans, and her strategy of conflation has successfully rubbed some of that appeal off onto her company.

What remains to be seen from Kylie's circumstances is the degree of tolerance that young consumers have for such a venture when its future diverges from that of its founder.

CHAPTER 6

A FUSION OF HERITAGE WITH MODERNITY

—

Tens of magazine covers with painted faces blink across a screen. Famous models with dewy skin, bold colors swiped across their eyes, and glossy lips stare at the viewer from the photographs. They are dressed as seventeenth-century Puritans, eighteenth-century French aristocrats, abstract versions of 1920s movie stars, and 1990s plastic surgery patients. Others have geometric shapes and smudges of neon pigment adorning their faces.

Next, a clip of a runway show flashes by, featuring models with spidery sliver lashes that extend to their temples and cheekbones. More models strut across the screen with gold trinkets, fabric, pearls, and Swarovski crystals pasted to their faces. One resembles a zombie out of the movie *Corpse Bride* while another is dressed as Nefertiti.

Rihanna and Kim Kardashian appear with intricate pieces of gold eye armor. Madonna glares and Oprah smiles. Punk teens with black makeup and spiked hair cross a street in Beatles-style formation. A 1960s pinup girl holds a bag between her open legs. A group of models exude joy as they dance.

This video is a compilation of makeup artist Pat McGrath's extraordinary creations throughout the decades. As a perfect encapsulation of her brand, it is uploaded on the website of her cosmetics company, Pat McGrath Labs.[107]

By the proclamation of *Vogue*'s Anna Wintour, Pat is the most influential makeup artist in the world.[108]

By the acknowledgment of Queen Elizabeth II, Pat is a member of the Order of the British Empire for services to the fashion and beauty industries.[109]

By the admiration of her friends and fans, Pat is "The Mother of Makeup."[110]

Her story as an artist and a businesswoman began in Northampton, England, where she was raised by a single mom who adored fashion and beauty. As British Jamaicans in the 1970s and 1980s, they struggled to find products that were suited for their dark skin. Pat disclosed in an interview with *Time*, "My earliest memories of makeup are rooted in

---

107 "About Pat McGrath Labs," Pat McGrath Labs, accessed May 29, 2020.
108 "Pat McGrath Biography," Pat McGrath Labs, accessed May 29, 2020.
109 Ibid.
110 Shannon Peter, "'The Mother of Make-up,' Pat Mcgrath, Reflects on Her Iconic Career," *i-D*, April 11, 2019.

experimentation—concocting new formulations, playing with different pigments to mix and match and blend and create something that matched my personal skin tone."[111]

Her passion lured her to London in the late 1980s, where she pursued a fashion degree by day.[112] By night, she frequently travelled to Paris to sneak into fashion shows under the guise of being a magazine editor.[113] This strategy enabled her to meet stylist Kim Bowen, who invited her on shoots for the magazines *The Face* and *i-D*. Eventually, Caron Wheeler, the lead singer of the pop group Soul II Soul, asked her to become her makeup artist on the group's Japanese tour.[114]

A legendary career began.

Pat spent ten seasons creating the makeup concepts for Prada and Miu Miu in the 1990s.[115] In 2004, Procter & Gamble named her Global Cosmetics Creative Design Director and placed her in charge of CoverGirl, Max Factor, and Dolce & Gabbana. She has worked on every cover and lead editorial story for *Vogue Italia* and has developed cosmetic lines for Giorgio Armani and Gucci. Every season, she creates makeup looks for more than sixty fashion shows in Milan, Paris, London, and New York.[116]

---

111 Cady Lang, "How Renowned Makeup Artist Pat McGrath Is Changing the Face of Beauty On Her Terms," *Time*, September 18, 2017.
112 Bibby Sowray, "Pat McGrath," *Vogue*, January 27, 2012.
113 Linda Wells, "Pat McGrath Is the Most In-Demand Makeup Artist in the World," *The Cut*, August 8, 2016.
114 Bibby Sowray, "Pat McGrath," *Vogue*, January 27, 2012.
115 Ibid.
116 "Pat McGrath Biography," Pat McGrath Labs, accessed May 29, 2020.

She also runs a billion-dollar cosmetics company.

Pat McGrath Labs traces its origins to spring 2015, when Pat acted on her Instagram followers' long-standing request to create products for them. She was experimenting with colors in a lab and accidentally formulated an intensely metallic gold pigment that enraptured her.[117] On September 30, the company launched with Gold 001 as its sole product. Advertised only on Pat's social media, all one thousand units sold out in six minutes.[118]

Three years and a permanent collection later, Pat McGrath Labs received a $60 million minority investment from Eurazeo Brands. This propelled the cosmetics company to unicorn status, prompting many on social media to argue that Pat was a better choice than Kylie Jenner to be on the cover of *Forbes* as a self-made billionaire.[119]

Pat McGrath Labs continued its growth, launching in Selfridges in April 2019. It achieved the highest cosmetics turnover in the first month out of any other brand in the department store's history. According to *The Guardian*, Selfridges sold a Pat McGrath Labs product every forty seconds in April.[120]

---

[117] Shannon Peter, "'The Mother of Make-up,' Pat Mcgrath, Reflects on Her Iconic Career," *i-D*, April 11, 2019.

[118] Sali Hughes, "Beauty Queen: How Pat McGrath Became the World's Most Influential Makeup Artist," *The Guardian*, August 6, 2017.

[119] Temi Adebowale, "Pat McGrath's Makeup Line Is Now Worth $1 Billion," *Harper's Bazaar*, July 20, 2018.

[120] Lisa Niven-Phillips, "Pat McGrath Labs Becomes Selfridges Biggest-Selling Beauty Line," *The Guardian*, June 1, 2019.

What is astonishing about Pat's business is its enormous appeal to young consumers. Much of the company's popularity stems from Millennial and Generation Z fans who follow its Instagram account and watch beauty influencers' reviews on its products.

How did this beauty veteran succeed in appealing to a new wave of enthusiasts who are largely divorced from editorial and runway culture?

The answer lies in her company's unique branding: Pat McGrath Labs symbolizes a fusion of heritage with modernity. Pat has created a company that preserves traditional elements of its founder's decades-long reputation while adapting perfectly to the current beauty context. The convergence of old and new that Pat McGrath Labs represents lends itself to beauty's version of nostalgia marketing, a tactic that has long been used by many industries to attract young audiences.

Kate Wolff, senior vice president of client services at marketing agency RQ, explained the allure of nostalgia marketing in an *Entrepreneur* article. She asserted that "today, nostalgia has a tight grip on Millennials…They've seen the birth of the internet, the rise of social media and the societal influx of virtual reality and artificial intelligence. At the same time, they've mourned the loss of CDs, photo books, film development, and video cassettes. They're the first age cohort to grow up with technology, and the last to remember life without it. As a result, they love to reminisce about how things *used to be*."

She also denotes a type of marketing nostalgia known as *fauxstalgia*, which is defined as a feeling of nostalgia toward a time period one did not actually live in. This phenomenon has worked wonders on Generation Z. For example, the Netflix show *Stranger Things*, the game *Pokémon Go*, and the vintage clothing and decorations sold at Urban Outfitters all incite fauxstalgia for eras that Generation Z did not personally experience.

As Kate explains, *Pokémon Go* linked the past with the present by maintaining the imagery of the original 1990s game on the new mobile platform. It therefore attracted Millennial *Pokémon* card collectors with nostalgia and Generation Z with fauxstalgia.[121]

The magic of Pat McGrath Labs is that the company intertwines this longing for the past with an adoration of the present. While it evokes nostalgia and fauxstalgia through its roots in Pat's career, it also embodies its founder's love for the innovation that the modern beauty community embraces. This paradoxical combination enables the company to deeply connect with young consumers on social media.

The most conspicuous example of this strategy lies in the company's Instagram marketing. The vision that Pat projects to her more than three million followers is a mélange of the contemporary and the historic.

---

121 Kate Wolff, "Beyond Nostalgia: How Brands Can Leverage the Powers of 'Fauxstalgia' and 'Newstalgia,'" *Entrepreneur*, January 14, 2019.

On one hand, Pat's Instagram page, which also serves as her company's account, reposts pictures of modern stars. Celebrities like Cardi B, Priyanka Chopra, Lil Nas X, Taylor Swift, Millie Bobby Brown, and Jennifer Lopez have appeared wearing Pat's products. Featured alongside them have been the young "muses" that Pat discovered through the platform, such as plus-size model Paloma Elsesser and drag queens Violet Chachki and Miss Fame.[122] Each of them has anywhere from hundreds of thousands to millions of followers, and they have all modeled Pat McGrath Labs products. In a true eschewing of tradition, Pat even named Lil Miquela, a computer-generated influencer who is a distinctly Generation Z phenomenon, as one of her muses.[123]

On the other hand, the company's Instagram account frequently elicits nostalgia and fauxstalgia among young consumers for the decades that formed or inspired Pat. For instance, she shares pictures and videos of icons like David Bowie, Tina Turner, and The Supremes. Interspersed between are images that are reminiscent of particular eras: a 1980s gold-plated cigarette lighter, a cherry-red 1970s Mercedes-Benz, a 1965 *Harper's Bazaar* shot of Jean Shrimpton dressed as an astronaut, Judy Garland's ruby red slippers from the 1939 *The Wizard of Oz*, zoomed-in details of Renaissance paintings.

One striking post features Freddie Mercury sitting on Darth Vader's shoulders in a 1980 concert at Wembley Arena.

---

122 Sali Hughes, "Beauty Queen: How Pat McGrath Became the World's Most Influential Makeup Artist," *The Guardian*, August 6, 2017.

123 Alexa Tietjen, "Influencer Ex Machina," *WWD*. July 11, 2018.

Another is of Carrie Fisher, dressed as Princess Leia, being hoisted into the air by Darth Vader. This photography is part of a series of *Star Wars*-themed posts that advertised Pat McGrath Labs's makeup collaboration with the franchise. Released at the end of December 2019, the collaboration promoted the movie *The Rise of Skywalker*. Much of the Instagram advertising for the collection mimicked the original *Star Wars* special effects and imagery, which conjured sentimentality for the franchise's early years.

In a more metaphorical way, Pat McGrath Labs products themselves also merge modernity with heritage. Their intensely vivid formulations are perfect for modern beauty enthusiasts, while their packaging evokes Pat's own past.

When Pat was rising to prominence in the 1990s, the mainstream of makeup was nude and subdued; it was her rejection of this status quo that propelled her to popularity. However, her daring and colorful looks incited industry experts to doubt her ability to appeal to everyday customers. As she stated in an interview with *The Guardian*, "I spoke to makeup executives about my own line for the past fifteen years and they'd say: 'You know, nobody knows you, nobody really wants the kind of stuff you do in shows in real life.' And then I joined social media and all I'd hear from thousands and thousands of people was that they did."[124]

With the explosion of YouTube and Instagram, beauty enthusiasts moved in the direction of fearless beauty that Pat had

---

124 Sali Hughes, "Beauty Queen: How Pat McGrath Became the World's Most Influential Makeup Artist," *The Guardian*, August 6, 2017.

been championing for decades. As viewers learned from influencers how to create adventurous looks, creativity and experimentation became the new norm.

Pat McGrath Labs taps into this daring beauty atmosphere of today with richly pigmented eyeshadows, gleaming highlighters, and bold lipsticks. These products are intense enough to show up on the deepest of skin tones, which allows every user to build a striking makeup look without much effort.

The quality of these particular products have not gone unnoticed in the beauty community. In fact, the widespread consensus is that Pat McGrath's eyeshadows and lipsticks are some of the most impactful in the industry.

For example, when influencer Jackie Aina reviewed Pat's $125 Mothership VI eyeshadow palette, she declared the following: "Now, we know Ms. Pat is upper-echelon [and] definitely not the starter-pack price range. But I can honestly say there is zero comparison to any other palettes on the market. The quality is just that impeccable." This YouTube video received more than half a million views.[125]

Another influencer, Tati Westbrook, shared a similar sentiment about the eyeshadows in a video that received more than one million views. While testing some of the shades on her arms, she claimed, "There's just not much else out there that has the richness of Pat's shadows."[126]

---

125 *Jackie Aina*, "Pat McGrath Has Done It Again?! MotherShip VI Demo," September 18, 2019, video, 16:02.
126 *Tati*, "$1,000 Pat McGrath Face," August 9, 2019, video, 24:45.

Furthermore, in a video that received over four million views, NikkieTutorials applauded the quality of Pat's matte lipsticks. She affirmed, "These are high-end lipsticks…[that] retail for $38. Now that is a lot of money for lipstick, money that I am willing to spend…because this is truly…one of the best lipstick formulas I've ever tried in my life."[127] Her endorsement of the formula is especially significant because Nikkie is known for her high standards for product opacity.

While the interior of Pat's products appeals to the present, the exterior symbolically evokes the history of Pat's career.

Notably, her packaging often features faces that are painted to look like creations straight out of an avant-garde runway show or an issue of *Vogue*. For example, her ten-pan eyeshadow palettes are housed in cardboard boxes decorated with ravishing images of women who look like extraterrestrial queens. The tone of each woman's makeup look and the hue of her skin, whether green, purple, or fuchsia, reflect the color scheme that is inside each palette.

Pat is selling more than makeup; like she has done in shoots and shows for decades, she is producing a concept. Every component is its own piece of art, feeding into the overarching brand theme of abstract astronomy. Together, the products speak to Pat's longstanding capacity to bring a canvas to life.

This legacy of artistic vision that subliminally fuels nostalgia and fauxstalgia is even more apparent when looking at the

---

127 *NikkieTutorials*, "World's Best Lipsticks," July 12, 2017, video, 16:45.

company's website. Under some of the products are a series of old paintings and photographs that served as inspiration for the packaging and color story. For example, twelve images accompany one of the newest Pat McGrath Labs eyeshadow palettes, Mothership VI: Midnight Sun. In these photographs, a 1970s Disco woman peers upward, two men from the 1980s New Romantic subculture pose, Grace Jones stares from a 1980 vinyl cover, and 1960s model Donyale Luna grins while clad in hammered gold adornments.

Every aspect of Pat McGrath Labs, from its visuals to its products, reinforces the company's branding as a union of old and new. Though this may not be consciously apparent to many consumers, it subliminally reinforces the reputation of the company as a modern enterprise fortified by decades of artistic expression, experience, and culture.

Pat's approach is rare in the beauty industry. Most other founders set their eye squarely toward the future as they compete to anticipate the next big fad in marketing and product development. After all, in an industry that is oversaturated and constantly evolving, it is critical for companies that appeal to Millennials and Generation Z to avoid being classified as "outdated."

However, as Pat McGrath Labs demonstrates, there is a way to fearlessly celebrate the past while standing at the cutting edge of innovation. Crucially, this kind of branding requires a founder who loves makeup experimentation as much as today's young beauty enthusiasts do. A venture that is built upon this foundation of passion can evoke nostalgia and fauxstalgia toward past eras without appearing stagnant or distant.

Though inspired by the runway and editorial traditions of the past, Pat can intuitively relate to young consumers because she shares their belief in the creativity of makeup. As a result of her innate appreciation of the beauty world that Millennials and Generation Z have built, she easily honors their vision of beauty while infusing it with her own sources of inspiration.[128]

Pat has long been waiting for this atmosphere. As she proclaims on her website, "This is the golden age of makeup. Pat McGrath Labs is my Golden Revolution. The entire planet is just as cosmetics obsessed as I've always been. Makeup is a movement. Makeup is mesmerizing. Makeup is *major*. Mantra-esque, three words have repeated over and over in my mind ever since I was young. Obsession. Inspiration. Addiction."[129]

Millennials and Generation Z have pushed the beauty industry to catch up to Pat's creed over the past decade, providing fertile soil for Pat McGrath Labs to flourish. What is most remarkable is the company's knack for recalling the aesthetic and cultural contexts that, though seemingly divorced from the current atmosphere, paved the way for the beauty industry of today.

---

[128] Cady Lang, "How Renowned Makeup Artist Pat McGrath Is Changing the Face of Beauty On Her Terms," *Time*, September 18, 2017.

[129] "About Pat McGrath Labs," Pat McGrath Labs, accessed May 29, 2020.

It was the act of navigating this old version of beauty, more niche and elitist than today's, that molded Pat into the paragon of artistry that she is. Her company simultaneously pays homage to this history, embraces the bravery and diversity of the present, and eagerly anticipates the future.

Through this endeavor, Pat has created a venture of makeup artistry that is timeless.

CHAPTER 7

BEWARE THE BUBBLE OF INFLUENCER MARKETING

In the summer of 2014, Morphe Brushes's website crashed due to an overwhelming influx of traffic. Customers had flocked to the website of the little-known cosmetics company after YouTube influencer Jaclyn Hill had recommended some of Morphe's $2 eyeshadows in one of her videos. Co-founder Linda Tawil immediately recognized the potential of this kind of marketing. She cleverly reached out to Jaclyn and offered her a 10 percent discount code for her subscribers to use, presumably also granting Jaclyn a commission from products bought using that code.[130]

The partnership that was consequently born has become a perfect case study of how influencers can propel an obscure company into the mainstream.

---

130 *Jaclyn Hill*, "August Beauty Favorites," September 4, 2014, video, 18:12.

Morphe Brushes, now known only as Morphe, was founded in 2008 by siblings Linda and Chris Tawil.[131] The company began as a trade show business, showcasing its small range of products to professionals at cosmetics exhibitions. As Linda recounted, "We set up, worked, and shut down our booths ourselves. Sometimes we'd take turns going to the smaller shows to try to give each other a little break. Chris drove our trade show setup and merchandise from state to state...to help save on shipping costs. There were times when he was away from home for a month at a time."[132]

Everything changed in 2014 when Jaclyn, an established influencer who had already worked with several cosmetics companies, introduced Morphe to her subscribers. In a video that received almost one million views, she held up a palette containing Morphe eyeshadows and claimed, "I would compare these to MAC eyeshadows."[133] At the time, the beauty community widely recognized MAC Cosmetics eyeshadows as some of the best on the market despite their hefty price tag. With this profound endorsement, Jaclyn became Morphe's first affiliate.

A chain reaction followed as more influencers realized the potential of this affordable company, which was already supported by Jaclyn, to appeal to young beauty enthusiasts. These YouTubers began to vouch for Morphe's products in

---

[131] Harry Brumpton, "General Atlantic Nears Acquisition of Beauty Brand Morphe," *Reuters*, July 18, 2019.

[132] "#BalanceForBetter: An Interview with the Co-Founders of Morphe," Lookfantastic, accessed May 30, 2020.

[133] *Jaclyn Hill*, "Update | Real Talk | A Little About Me | Haters | Makeup Talk," August 19, 2014, video, 18:40.

front of millions of viewers, suggesting that they rivaled those from much more expensive companies like MAC and Makeup Geek. Morphe took note, inviting these influencers to be affiliates. They received unique discount codes for their subscribers to use when purchasing from the Morphe website, and for each of those sales, they earned a commission.

In the midst of this overwhelmingly positive response, some pushback began to appear. For example, Tati Westbrook remarked in a video with over one million views that Morphe's matte eyeshadows were difficult to blend. She stated, "To be honest, my immediate thought was…'Oh my god, am I missing something?' What is the hype? What is the big fuss about this? I just don't understand."[134]

This sentiment was reflected by many consumers who purchased from the company. They posted comments under YouTube videos, sharing that their eyeshadows performed poorly and that the brushes quickly fell apart.

Nonetheless, Morphe's robust affiliate program, the backbone of its marketing, ensured that the company was exceedingly well-received by the beauty community. Across YouTube, influencers recommended its products in their videos before flashing their discount codes across the screen. They also inserted unique affiliate links to Morphe's website in the description of their videos, which tracked the traffic that each influencer sent to the website and the purchases

---

134 *Tati*, "Morphe Makeup & Brushes | Hot or Not," December 17, 2015, video, 13:20.

that customers subsequently made.[135] The commissions that they earned from each sale continually fueled the frenzy of endorsements. Since influencers typically did not disclose that they were profiting off of their codes and links, young viewers were none the wiser.[136]

Although the Tawils were outsiders to the beauty community, Morphe exploded onto the YouTube scene because of strategic partnerships with these influencers, referred to as "Morphe Babes." According to Linda, "One thing that sets Morphe apart are our Morphe Babes. They truly are our family, and we wouldn't have made it this far without all their love and support."[137]

The motivation for these YouTubers is clear: Morphe's prices enabled them to reach the wallets of a wide selection of young viewers. After all, most teenagers could put together a few dollars for some eyeshadows and brushes. By recommending items with affordable prices, influencers sold such a large volume of Morphe items that their commissions dwarfed what they would earn when advertising products from expensive companies.

Morphe's bestsellers became its $23 palettes containing thirty-five eyeshadows, resulting in a cost per eyeshadow of $0.66. This was a fraction of the price of eyeshadows sold by

---

135 *Smokey Glow*, "The Truth About Affiliate Links," April 28, 2020, video, 22:31.

136 *Amandab*, "How Morphe Brushes Changed the Beauty Industry ... (The Problem With Morphe)," March 6, 2020, video, 36:27.

137 "#BalanceForBetter: An Interview with the Co-Founders of Morphe," Lookfantastic, accessed May 30, 2020.

other mainstream beauty businesses. However, the cost is not so astounding when considering that lesser known online companies like Sedona Lace and AliExpress were offering palettes with one hundred twenty eyeshadows that were also around $23.

But, what *was* unique about Morphe is the legitimacy gained from beauty influencers' promotion. Jaclyn's continued backing provided a precedent for other influencers to laud Morphe's quality, and the company encouraged this endless praise by making them affiliates and sending them waves of free products. Influencer endorsement made all the difference. Sedona Lace and AliExpress were viewed as *cheap* businesses with dry formulas intended for children, and they were rarely mentioned by established YouTube influencers. In contrast, Morphe became known for *affordable* palettes that competed in a higher league.

This kind of intense influencer marketing created an exaggerated bubble of hype. In this situation, consumers were so inundated by too-good-to-be true Morphe reviews that any major setback would mean betrayal and a burst bubble.

The pin arrived in 2016.

It came in the form of the YouTube video "Morphe Brand Review," uploaded by beauty manufacturing professional Stephanie Nicole. During the course of the video, she demonstrated how to use Morphe's ingredient lists to research its formulas' originality. In front of almost two million viewers, she proved that Morphe has almost the same eyeshadow formula as Crown Brushes, Sedona Lace, AliExpress, Makeup

Artist Network, and Bella Face. These were the "cheap" companies that the YouTube beauty community had generally avoided. Stephanie also argued that Morphe purchased its eyeshadows and brushes from Crown Brushes, which had its own factory in China. Morphe would then stamp its own name on the products and resell them on its website for a higher price.[138]

This practice of one company purchasing another's products, modifying them slightly, and marketing them as their own is known as private labelling. As Stephanie explained in the case of brushes, creating original products is expensive: "You would have to own your own factory that's going to get all of these pieces, and…machines that can put all the hair together in the ferrule, and pinch it, and glue it, and print [the name]. It's a huge cost undertaking." Therefore, it is not unusual for new companies to go this route until they can invest in their own products.[139]

However, Morphe was not an unknown venture trying to gain a foothold in the industry. For more than a year, the Tawils had been ingeniously convincing young beauty enthusiasts that their company was a comparable alternative to high-quality competitors. "They were playing chess with us," declared Amanda Elimian in a YouTube video titled "How Morphe Brushes Changed the Beauty Industry."[140] But Stephanie's revelation exposed the ruse.

---

138 *Stephanie Nicole*, "Morphe Brand Review," February 23, 2016, video, 25:08.

139 Ibid.

140 *Amandabb*, "How Morphe Brushes Changed the Beauty Industry … (The Problem With Morphe)," March 6, 2020, video, 36:27.

Morphe's rose-colored mirage dissipated as news spread that its formulas were almost identical to those of poor-quality products. Consumers who already felt bombarded by the affiliate marketing decided that it was all too much. Beauty audiences began to distrust YouTubers who gushed over Morphe products before mentioning their discount codes and affiliate links.[141] In response, influencers across the platform dramatically scaled back their overt recommendations of the company's products in an attempt to preserve their relationship with subscribers.

As a result of this general abatement of hype, Morphe has had to leverage influencers in new ways.

It currently partners with other companies by selling their products on the Morphe website and in Morphe stores. Its partners include influencer-founded ventures like Jeffree Star Cosmetics, Jaclyn Cosmetics, Dominique Cosmetics, and Lunar Beauty. Morphe provides these otherwise online-only companies retail space in its stores, allowing the influencers' subscribers to test the products and see the promotional pictures in-person.

When Morphe launches its own products, its marketing strategy now revolves around inviting influencers to collaborate on them. Jaclyn Hill, James Charles, Jeffree Star, Bretman Rock, and Manny MUA have all produced their own palettes and brush sets with Morphe that have excited their audiences of millions. By linking each item with a specific influencer,

---

141 Micaela, "Banking on the Influencer Empire: Meet Morphe Cosmetics," Medium, March 11, 2019.

the company encourages consumers to relate to the products on a personal level.

When James Charles announced on YouTube that he had created a collection with Morphe consisting of a rainbow eyeshadow palette and brush set, his video received over eleven million views.[142] For the primarily Generation Z fans who adore James, purchasing his palette is a means of relating to him, partaking in his subscriber culture of more than twenty million people, and supporting his artistry. Unsurprisingly, the collection sold out in less than ten minutes when it launched in November 2018 and it continued to sell out for four subsequent restocks.[143] [144]

Morphe has maintained its self-proclaimed identity as "a beauty brand created for the creators," but it is no longer operating within the frenzy of a bubble.[145] Gone are exaggerated and overwhelming inundations of positive Morphe videos. In fact, major influencers typically only review Morphe when it releases product collaborations with other YouTubers.

When there is an issue, the community is less likely to gloss over the problem as it was in the past.

---

142 *James Charles*, "James Charles x Morphe Reveal," November 2, 2018, video, 36:28.

143 Elisabeth Mansson, "Sister Stocked? Not A Chance. The James Charles x Morphe Palette Has Sold Out For A Second Time," TheTalko, December 13, 2018.

144 Micaela, "Banking on the Influencer Empire: Meet Morphe Cosmetics," Medium, March 11, 2019.

145 "About Morphe," Morphe, accessed May 30, 2020.

For example, when Jaclyn Hill and Morphe partnered in the summer of 2018 to launch a collection of four eyeshadow palettes, they were the subject of extended controversy. The collection was sent out to YouTubers to review right before it went up for sale, and problems immediately began to emerge. Influencer Jackie Aina tested the palettes in a video, and more than one million viewers saw her try to build up the intensity of one eyeshadow only to have the powder completely dust off her lid. The comments section of that video was filled with viewers' complaints about the poor quality of the products.[146]

The uproar was so significant that Morphe and Jaclyn decided to postpone the launch for a few weeks until the quality of the eyeshadows could be improved.[147] This spurred Makeup Geek CEO Marlena Stell to chime in, arguing in a now-deleted tweet that it is logistically impossible for a company whose products are manufactured in China to re-press the eyeshadows into palettes and ship to the United States within the postponement period.

Morphe's reputation is still recovering, though it has ridden the influencer train to tremendous financial success. In August 2019, private equity firm General Atlantic announced that it will acquire a majority stake in Morphe, joining

---

146 *Jackie Aina*, "Jaclyn Hill x Morphe Vault: They Almost Had Me In the First Half Not Gonna Lie," June 17, 2018, video, 17:42.

147 Laura Capon, "Morphe Has Delayed the Launch of Their Jaclyn Hill Vault Collection after Poor YouTube Reviews," *Cosmopolitan*, June 22, 2018.

existing investor Summit Partners.¹⁴⁸ *Reuters* reported that the deal will value the company at more than $2 billion.¹⁴⁹

Nonetheless, the cosmetics company has lost respectability in the eyes of many beauty lovers, and influencers are visibly wary of promoting its products like they did in the past.

In part due to the drama around Morphe, consumers of today are much more informed than they were during the early days of beauty's digital explosion. They understand that many influencers are forced to rely on sponsorships, discount codes, and affiliate links to earn their income, but consumers also expect a degree of integrity from them.

When I interviewed Leanne Almeida, an English major at Georgetown University, she explained this sentiment further: "I'd definitely be more likely to buy something that influencers are advertising if they don't advertise frequently and if…I was confident that they are careful about the endorsements that they want to put out into the world."

The key lesson to glean from Morphe's case is that influencer-based marketing must be used strategically and authentically. There is significant value in affordable cosmetics, particularly for young beauty enthusiasts who are looking to experiment with an abundance of colors without emptying their bank accounts. However, Morphe was not marketed in this realistic way; instead, influencers unleashed torrents of

---

148 "Morphe Holdings and General Atlantic Announce Partnership and Strategic Growth Investment," General Atlantic, August 19, 2019.

149 Harry Brumpton, "General Atlantic Nears Acquisition of Beauty Brand Morphe," *Reuters*, July 18, 2019.

hyperbolic endorsements that did not reflect the quality of the products that they held up to their cameras. When information materialized that the Tawils had chosen to invest in this misleading marketing at the expense of improving their formulas, Morphe's reputation was significantly tarnished.

Although influencers have the potential to elevate unknown companies onto the mainstream, care must be taken to preserve the trust between young viewers and influencers. If that trust erodes through disingenuous claims, viewers increasingly scrutinize subsequent endorsements, and influencers become unwilling to continue to vouch for the company. After all, one of the worst accusations with which an influencer must grapple is that she has been "bought" by a business and is no longer credible.

A true archetype of a YouTube-born venture, Morphe serves as a warning to the rest the industry. An influencer-led marketing bubble may provide legitimacy in the short term, but unsubstantiated claims render the bubble temporary and risky. Ultimately, Morphe's current financial prosperity will not mean much if its logo persistently reminds future users of deception and scandal.

CHAPTER 8

MAKE EVERY PLATFORM MATTER

In 2009, Huda Kattan was searching for a way to crack into the beauty industry. She was a recent finance graduate of the University of Michigan, but she had just moved to Dubai and wanted to pursue something radically different: makeup artistry.[150] With few connections and limited financial means, she started a blog so that she could build a client base. Little did she know, the *Huda Beauty Blog* would set Huda on a path to ubiquity.

A decade later, she is the CEO of a billion-dollar cosmetics business named Huda Beauty.

The company, born out of the popular blog, is a product of its founder's innate understanding of social media. In the past decade, Huda has built a 360-degree marketing strategy

---

[150] *Huda Beauty*, "My Makeup Business Story," October 6, 2016, video, 14:14.

that effectively reaches its global consumer base through all platforms.

The story of her success began in 2010 when she first launched the blog. At the time, it was rare to find professional makeup artists who shared their knowledge for free online.[151] The YouTube beauty community was still in its nascent stage, and Huda recognized the need for a space to share techniques and foster conversations around makeup. When she established her blog as a one-stop shop for beauty advice, she filled a niche in an industry that was just beginning its transformation.

Attracting an international following came naturally to her. An Iraqi-American, Huda was particularly well-poised to connect with both Western and Middle Eastern beauty enthusiasts. She had already become a makeup artist for Revlon Middle East, and she was introduced to Middle Eastern royalty when a sheikha from Abu Dhabi became one of her clients.[152] [153] She also looked to Facebook to diversify her audience, paying for $10 ads that targeted people from different countries and directed them to her blog.[154]

Soon, the blog was receiving a million views per month, and Huda wanted to take her connection with her viewers a step

---

151 Tamara Pupic, "How Huda, Mona, And Alya Kattan Built Huda Beauty Out Of Dubai," *Entrepreneur*, August 18, 2019.

152 "Huda Kattan," LinkedIn, accessed May 30, 2020.

153 Tamara Pupic, "How Huda, Mona, And Alya Kattan Built Huda Beauty Out Of Dubai," *Entrepreneur*, August 18, 2019.

154 Max Zahn, "How Beauty Influencer Huda Kattan Learned to Create Viral Posts," Yahoo! Finance, November 7, 2019.

further.[155] She explained in a 2018 speech at Harvard University, "We asked our community what they wanted from us. The response was overwhelming: products. They wanted a piece of us in the form of products."[156]

Huda listened and produced. Using her existing social media presence as a springboard, she dived into entrepreneurship with the launch of false eyelashes in 2011.

The first batch of eyelashes were modeled after Huda's own method of lash customization. She had become known for altering false eyelashes to match her eye shape, so she decided to make her creations available for sale to her followers. Huda paid for the first lashes with $10,000 from her own savings and $6,000 that her oldest sister Alya invested. Her backup plan if the eyelashes did not sell was to keep them as a lifetime supply for personal use.[157] [158]

When it came time to pitch her idea to Sephora Dubai Mall, Huda's existing relationship with her audience on *Huda Beauty Blog* provided a foundation of credibility. Artemis Patrick, senior vice president of merchandising at Sephora, revealed that the retail giant decided to launch Huda's eyelashes because her experience as a celebrity makeup artist

---

155 Huda Kattan, "Meet the CEO Who Turned a Makeup Hobby into a Multimillion Dollar Business," Chase, July 25, 2018.

156 *Huda Beauty*, "My Story through Feminism! We Should All be Feminist," December 5, 2018, video, 14:43.

157 Chloe Sorvino, "How Huda Kattan Built A Billion-Dollar Cosmetics Brand With 26 Million Followers," *Forbes*, July 11, 2018.

158 *Huda Beauty*, "My Makeup Business Story," October 6, 2016, video, 14:14.

with a prominent blog gave her an edge over traditional beauty companies.[159]

Even so, Sephora doubted her capacity to draw in masses of customers. According to an interview that Huda gave in *Entrepreneur*, Sephora Dubai Mall expected to sell around seven thousand units of Huda's lashes in a year after comparing them with lashes from other companies already sold in-store.

"They told us that we were a no-name, but we blew the numbers, we blew the established brands, and on the first day only, I think, we sold two thousand lashes," declared Huda. "There were not many press who featured us back then…because, at the time, no one knew what bloggers would become. It was a weird time for us, to be honest, because it was one of the very first times that an influencer was releasing a product."

By the end of *the first week*, seven thousand units had been sold.[160]

Allure wrote, "Kattan is known as the woman who sold Sephora on false eyelashes…They became a runway hit in the Middle East and the States, even landing on the lids of Kim Kardashian."[161] Huda Beauty the blog had become Huda Beauty the cosmetics company.

---

[159] Sheila McClear, "Why Huda Kattan Is One of Beauty's Most Influential Women," *Allure*, June 28, 2017.

[160] Tamara Pupic, "How Huda, Mona, And Alya Kattan Built Huda Beauty Out Of Dubai," *Entrepreneur*, August 18, 2019.

[161] Sheila McClear, "Why Huda Kattan Is One of Beauty's Most Influential Women," *Allure*, June 28, 2017.

The first year after launch drastically elevated Huda's marketing reach and enabled her to craft an outreach blueprint centered around community. She increased Huda Beauty's Instagram followers from eighty thousand to more than three million, creating an expansive base of supporters who fueled her early success.[162]

Instagram continues to be Huda's primary advertising channel. The company's account boasts more than forty-four million followers, an amount that enabled Huda to top Instagram's annual "Influencer Rich List" from 2017 to 2019 as the highest-earning beauty influencer on the platform.[163,164,165]

One of the principal reasons for the account's popularity is its regular feature of makeup influencers who use Huda Beauty items. These artists create stunning makeup looks with the products and they post the images to their own accounts for their audiences to see. Huda Beauty then reposts some of the pictures to the company's page, providing the artists with the massive exposure of forty-four million followers in exchange for the free product publicity. When consumers see influencers who they recognize executing beautiful looks with Huda's products, Huda Beauty's credibility on Instagram rises.

---

162 Huda Kattan, "Meet the CEO Who Turned a Makeup Hobby into a Multimillion Dollar Business," Chase, July 25, 2018.

163 "Instagram Rich List 2017—The Platform's Highest-Earners Revealed," Hopper HQ, November 10, 2017.

164 Laura Capon, "This Is the Beauty Influencer Who Topped This Year's Instagram Rich List," *Cosmopolitan*, July 24, 2018.

165 "Instagram Rich List 2019—Beauty Influencers," Hopper HQ, accessed May 30, 2020.

The company also threads humor into its Instagram posts, further attracting young followers. Among the traditional marketing posts, it often mixes in viral memes, videos of influencers trying crazy beauty fads, and clips of babies playing with beauty products. For instance, one hilarious reposted video is from a girl who drew an eye on her boyfriend's leg and applied mascara on his leg hair to mimic eyelashes around the eye. Another video shows a cat relaxing as it receives a head massage from an electric massage tool. Since the account has at least two new posts and multiple "story" videos a day, there is ample opportunity to fuse this light-heartedness with serious marketing.

On one occasion, the company's Instagram account even included its followers in the product formulation process. When Huda began to develop her Faux Filter Foundation, she sought to create a feeling of reciprocity within her community; the fans could voice the attributes that they desired in an ideal complexion product, and the company would listen. Huda explained in *The Guardian*, "I reached out to our Instagram audience because I wanted to understand what kind of coverage and [texture] they wanted and how they chose foundation. We had thousands of responses that helped guide us."[166]

Faux Filter refers to the foundation's high coverage formula, which is intended to act as an Instagram filter that blurs out skin imperfections. The YouTube reviews that emerged about the product confirmed its opacity. As influencer

---

166 Saba Imtiaz, "All Made up! The Indie Makeup Brands That Are Catering to Women of Colour," *The Guardian*, October 30, 2017.

NikkieTutorials claimed in a video that has been watched more than five million times, the foundation "leaves the skin looking 'plastic-fantastic'...it's like a veil of flawless, perfect skin."[167] This kind of formula was truly born out of the "full coverage" trend that exists on Instagram.

With these approaches, the Huda Beauty Instagram page has become an engaging, enjoyable, and informative platform. Followers come to the page not only to see how Huda's products can be used, but also to gain inspiration from diverse artists, learn new techniques, and laugh at jokes with fellow beauty lovers. With this kind of exposure to the company, their purchases of Huda Beauty products feel "more emotional than transactional."[168]

Beyond Instagram, Huda ensures that her YouTube presence allows her quirkiness to shine more extensively than it does on other platforms. The Huda Beauty YouTube channel, which has more than four million subscribers, combines makeup education with Huda's creative personality. For instance, its second-most watched video features Huda doing her elaborate hair, skincare, and makeup routines in the first-class section of an airplane. When viewers teased her about the luxuries of first-class, she released another video repeating the steps while sitting in the economy section.

Huda elucidated her YouTube strategy in a speech that she gave titled "The Power of Being Yourself" at one *The Business*

---

[167] *NikkieTutorials*, "Holy Grail Foundation? Huda Beauty Faux Filter Foundation Review," November 9, 2017, video, 15:56.

[168] Saba Imtiaz, "All Made up! The Indie Makeup Brands That Are Catering to Women of Colour," *The Guardian*, October 30, 2017.

of Fashion conference. When answering the question of how her company not only competed but dominated in the industry with few resources at her disposal, she explained, "When I became unapologetically myself, the weird, the awkward, the passionate Huda, our brand changed...People looked at me strange when I would say things like 'Can we do a blog on YouTube of me trying Vagisil, milk of magnesium, and KY Jelly as primer?'...[but] the impact was so profound."[169] Embracing her magnetic individuality enabled her to craft an appealing brand that easily distinguishes itself from traditional conglomerates, which take a more conventional approach to beauty.

Besides her quirkiness, her videos also show a more relatable side. Her third-most popular video to date is one called "How to Shave Your Face (And Why It's Awesome)," which has a thumbnail of Huda's face covered in shaving cream. This video was published in 2016, before most beauty influencers on YouTube spoke of face shaving for women.[170] Instead of fearing the stigma of vouching for a traditionally masculine routine, she identified an unmet educational need for women on the platform and brought a routine onto the conversational mainstream.

Lastly, Huda's YouTube channel emphasizes her family-oriented experience with business. Huda Beauty is run by the Kattan family, with Huda's husband Chris serving as chief operating officer, her sister Mona as global president, and

---

[169] *The Business of Fashion*, "Huda Kattan | The Power of Being Yourself," December 4, 2018, video, 9:54.

[170] *Huda Beauty*, "How to Shave Your Face (And Why It's Awesome)," April 11, 2016, video, 4:39.

her sister Ayla as chief Instagram officer.[171] The entire family, including Huda's young daughter, frequently stars in YouTube videos and unabashedly shows their personalities to viewers. This has allowed the family to portray a personalized vision of the brand. In fact, some of Huda's most-watched videos feature glimpses into her relationships and daily life at the company's office.

Despite the enormous success of Instagram and YouTube, Huda has not abandoned Facebook. In 2018, she starred in her own reality web series on Facebook Watch called *Huda Boss*, which chronicles the adventures of the Kattan family as it runs a cosmetics empire. Multiple episodes in the first season each received almost ten million views, prompting a subsequent season to roll out in 2019. Each episode in the second season also received several million views.

For a more professional side, Huda's Twitter provides links to the interviews and presentations that she consistently gives with major magazines and news networks. She even has a matte lipstick shade named "Interview," which is described as a *confident* peachy nude.

In 2019, Huda added another platform to her marketing portfolio: TikTok, a karaoke-style app that predominantly targets Generation Z. Huda Beauty is currently one of the few companies to produce content for the platform, which skyrocketed in popularity throughout the world in 2019. In a true ode to the youngest members of Generation Z, the

---

171 Tamara Pupic, "How Huda, Mona, And Alya Kattan Built Huda Beauty Out Of Dubai," *Entrepreneur*, August 18, 2019.

company has released videos of people using Huda's products to make shimmery slime.

In other words, Huda is an expert at being everywhere.

Her success lies in her ability to tailor content to each of the different platforms that Generation Z and Millennials use. Beginning with her blog, she has created a global community that can engage with the company through every social media avenue possible.

A vital characteristic to note about Huda Beauty's 360-degree marketing is its intentional appeal to both Middle Eastern and Western consumers.

Her company's Instagram feed is filled with beauty influencers of a variety of different backgrounds, including many Muslim women who cover their hair. On YouTube, she vacillates between uploading videos in English with Arabic subtitles and in Arabic with English subtitles. She has also collaborated on videos with well-known Middle Eastern-based YouTubers like Noor Stars, Mo Vlogs, and Nawras Sattar and with American YouTubers like Liza Koshy and Nikita Dragun. Each of them has an enormous audience of millions of subscribers.

Huda's products also target both demographics. While many of them are named after American pop culture phrases such as "Boujee," "Bawse," and "Dirty Thirty," some collections specifically honor the Middle East. According to the *Associated Press*, "Unlike in many Western countries where more natural makeup looks are in vogue, women across Arab Gulf countries often lean toward bright, eye-catching makeup trends and accessories that offset the utilitarianism of black veils and abayas."[172] This preference complements the bold colors of Huda Beauty's products. Huda even created an eyeshadow palette called "Desert Dusk," which is inspired by the colors of an Arabian desert in the moments after the sun has set.

As Sephora's Artemis Patrick affirmed, "It's rare for one person to be relatable across so many countries and cultures... Obviously, it's the power of the internet, but it's a testament to her business acumen that she can translate and harness the power of her followers."[173]

This cross-cultural appeal bolsters the objective that Huda shared on Girlboss Radio: she wants to be the Estée Lauder of the twenty-first century.[174]

Euromonitor International reported that from 2018 to 2023, there will be a predicted 7.2 percent growth in the color cosmetics industry across the Middle East. In 2019, the color cosmetics market was valued at $2.3 billion in the region, predicted to grow to $3.1 billion by 2023.[175]

---

172 Malak Harb, "For Huda Kattan, Beauty Has Become a Billion-Dollar Business," *The Associated Press*, October 13, 2019.

173 Bee Shapiro, "Is Huda Kattan the Most Influential Beauty Blogger in the World," *The New York Times*, March 20, 2017.

174 Sophia Amoruso and Huda Kattan, "How to Build a Billion-Dollar Company in 5 Years, According to a Beauty Founder," *Business Insider*, October 2, 2019.

175 Malak Harb, "For Huda Kattan, Beauty Has Become a Billion-Dollar Business," *The Associated Press*, October 13, 2019.

While many beauty conglomerates have long excluded Muslim women from their advertising, particularly those who wear veils, Huda's brand is built upon a foundation that celebrates the Middle East at its core. Huda Beauty can therefore dominate this market in a way that other companies struggle to mimic.

With the convergence of these diverse components of its 360-degree marketing strategy, Huda Beauty has been able to scale at an unprecedented rate. Within ten years of its birth, the company expanded to sell 213 makeup products ranging from eyeshadow palettes to face products to lipsticks. It also has a fragrance sub-brand named Kayali and a skincare sub-brand named Wishful.[176] Meanwhile, Huda claims to have spent essentially no money on advertising.[177]

Even more astounding is the fact that Huda Beauty only accepted a single outside investor among the many who have submitted offers. This investor, the private equity firm TSG Consumer Partners, acquired a small minority stake at the end of 2017, which valued the company at $1.2 billion according to *Forbes*.[178]

When asked in an interview with Yahoo! Finance about the possibility of future investments, Mona Kattan divulged that the company will probably go the initial public offering (IPO) route that would launch the company into the stock

---

176 Tamara Pupic, "How Huda, Mona, And Alya Kattan Built Huda Beauty Out Of Dubai," *Entrepreneur*, August 18, 2019.

177 "Huda Kattan," *Forbes*, September 3, 2019.

178 Ibid.

market.[179] By planning to raise capital from public investors, the Kattan sisters exude a self-assured attitude that they can appeal to the masses. This is the ultimate show of confidence for Huda Beauty's extensive reach.

Huda Beauty is an archetype of an online company that expertly leverages every kind of social media avenue to build a community of millions. Bolstered by a creative founder who innately understands how to market her content to young consumers, Huda Beauty is a venture that transcends platforms and cultures.

---

179 Max Zahn, "How Beauty Influencer Huda Kattan Learned to Create Viral Posts," Yahoo! Finance, November 7, 2019.

CHAPTER 9

THE AGE OF CLEAN BEAUTY

In April 2018, Calabasas reality TV culture collided with Washington, D.C.'s neoclassical scene. Clad in a black pantsuit, Kourtney Kardashian ventured to Congress to push for a cleaner approach to beauty. She threw her support behind the bipartisan Personal Care Products Safety Act, which would have empowered the United States Food and Drug Administration (FDA) to prevent the sales of dangerous cosmetics. More than one million people liked the Instagram post she made about her trip, and news media commended her for calling attention to the issue.[180]

Kourtney is emblematic of a larger atmosphere of ingredient distrust among American consumers, spurred by the FDA's notoriously weak regulation of the beauty industry.

---

180 Jeffrey Cook, "Kourtney Kardashian Arrives on Capitol Hill to Clean up Cosmetics," *ABC News*, April 24, 2018.

According to the 2019 Women's Facial Skincare Consumer Report from market research company The NPD Group, 46 percent of facial skincare users report purchasing products free of sulfates, phthalates, and/or gluten. This is a 6 percent increase from just two years prior. The survey also found that more than 50 percent of women look for skincare products made from organic ingredients.[181]

Despite the fact that beauty products have drastically evolved to include complex formulations with powerful ingredients, the FDA still operates by the lenient framework of the Federal Food, Drug, and Cosmetic Act of 1938. The only ingredients that the agency regulates in cosmetics are color additives, while the rest are exempt from its oversight. To make matters worse, the FDA is not authorized to order recalls in the case of hazardous cosmetics; it is up to manufacturers to voluntarily ask customers to return dangerous products or to discard them.[182] [183]

Often, cosmetics companies step up to the plate and undergo their own rigorous testing of ingredients. After all, it is in their interest to maintain a trustworthy reputation among consumers.

---

[181] "Empowered Consumers Want Clean Ingredients and Brand Transparency from Skincare Products," The NPD Group, August 14, 2019.

[182] "Statement from FDA Commissioner Scott Gottlieb, M.D., and Susan Mayne, Ph.D., Director of the Center for Food Safety and Applied Nutrition, on Tests Confirming a 2017 Finding of Asbestos Contamination in Certain Cosmetic Products and New Steps That FDA Is Pursuing to Improve Cosmetics Safety," US Food and Drug Administration, March 5, 2019.

[183] Molly Wanner and Neera Nathan, "Clean Cosmetics: The Science behind the Trend," Harvard Health Publishing: Harvard Medical School, March 4, 2019.

Additionally, according to Dr. Molly Wanner and Dr. Neera Nathan from Harvard Health Publishing, although "scientific evidence appears to support avoiding at least a handful of ingredients that could be lurking in your personal care products, including MI/MCI, fragrance mix, and formaldehyde ... more studies are needed to back up associations between low-dose topical exposure to many of these chemicals and human health."[184]

However, American consumers remain wary.

This is unsurprising given the regulations passed by other governments. For instance, the European Union has banned or restricted more than 1,300 cosmetic chemicals believed to cause health problems. By comparison, the United States has outlawed or limited only eleven cosmetic chemicals.[185]

The ingredient alarm is also to be expected in the wake of a 2017 incident in which Claire's makeup for children tested positive for tremolite asbestos, which is extremely toxic if swallowed or inhaled. The tests were conducted at an independent lab on behalf of Kristi Warner, a Rhode Island mom and attorney who was concerned about the chemicals in her young daughter's makeup. After the news broke, Claire's removed the items from its shelves.[186]

---

184 Ibid.

185 Oliver Milman, "US Cosmetics Are Full of Chemicals Banned by Europe—Why," *The Guardian*, May 22, 2019.

186 Emily Volz, "Consumer Advocate: Claire's Pulls Children's Makeup after Family Finds Asbestos," *WJAR*, December 22, 2017.

When the FDA completed its own testing of the products in 2019, it issued a warning that three of them did indeed contain asbestos and that customers should immediately cease use. Moreover, the FDA "requested that Claire's recall the products…[but] Claire's has refused to comply…and the agency does not have authority to mandate a recall."[187], [188]

In this atmosphere, consumers across the board are paying more attention to ingredients. The NPD report has found that "brands making a public commitment to ingredient transparency have become top-of-mind for consumers, with several of the more well-known transparent brands ranking among the Top 25 in highest awareness-to-purchase conversions."[189] This conversion indicates the rate at which people make a purchase from a particular company after becoming aware of its existence.

When I interviewed Grace Shin, a corporate accounting and finance major at Bentley University, she expressed a common sentiment felt by skincare enthusiasts: "We can't just consume blindly; if we are going to use these products on our faces daily, we have to look at what they are composed of."

---

187 "FDA Advises Consumers to Stop Using Certain Cosmetic Products," US Food and Drug Administration, October 18, 2019.

188 "Statement from FDA Commissioner Scott Gottlieb, M.D., and Susan Mayne, Ph.D., Director of the Center for Food Safety and Applied Nutrition, on Tests Confirming a 2017 Finding of Asbestos Contamination in Certain Cosmetic Products and New Steps That FDA Is Pursuing to Improve Cosmetics Safety," US Food and Drug Administration, March 5, 2019.

189 "Empowered Consumers Want Clean Ingredients and Brand Transparency from Skincare Products," The NPD Group, August 14, 2019.

Enter Drunk Elephant.

The company is a pioneer of the clean cosmetics movement and called for safer ingredients even before the word "clean" became an industry buzzword. It was launched by stay-at-home mom Tiffany Masterson in August 2013 with the objective of developing skincare products devoid of any questionable ingredients.[190] A believer in the efficacy of marula oil, she named the company after a myth that elephants get drunk from eating the fruit of marula trees.[191]

Its products are free of what Tiffany deems the "suspicious six": essential oils, drying alcohols, silicones, chemical sunscreens, fragrances, and sodium lauryl sulfate. Those ingredients irritated her skin for years until she eliminated them entirely from her routine. Since she struggled to find formulas on the market that did not contain the suspicious six, she decided to make her own products that would meet her standard.[192]

Tiffany defines a "clean" ingredient as one that does not cause disease or disruption to the body when it "penetrates the skin and enters into the bloodstream. In other words, clean means safe for the body."[193] However, as she explained in a *Forbes*

---

190 Joanna Fu, "Drunk Elephant Founder Tiffany Masterson on Her 'Suspicious 6' Skincare Philosophy," *Vogue*, November 26, 2019.

191 Nora Maloney, "Drunk Elephant Founder Tiffany Masterson Takes Skincare by Storm," *Vanity Fair*, January 10, 2018.

192 Tiffany Masterson, "Founder Note," Drunk Elephant, accessed May 30, 2020.

193 Joanna Fu, "Drunk Elephant Founder Tiffany Masterson on Her 'Suspicious 6' Skincare Philosophy," *Vogue*, November 26, 2019.

interview, "the 'clean' beauty industry has been diluted to the point that it's hard to know what it means anymore. Everyone is doing it and there is no regulation around it. It's whatever a brand decides it is, which is completely inconsistent and confusing to the consumer."[194]

As a result, Tiffany never explicitly branded Drunk Elephant as a "clean beauty" company. Instead, she created a new category: "clean-compatible."

Clean-compatibility indicates that the company removes all ingredients that are *potentially* disruptive to the skin organ. In other words, it takes the "clean" label a step further because Tiffany does not "think clean is enough if you want healthy, balanced skin."[195] Her focus is on creating products that are biocompatible with skin, which means that their formulas contain non-irritating, small-molecule ingredients that are easily absorbed.[196] As she told *Vogue*, "all biocompatible ingredients are clean, but not all clean ingredients are compatible and beneficial for skin."[197]

Tiffany also draws a distinction between "clean-compatible" and "natural."

---

194 Karin Eldor, "Drunk Elephant's Founder Shares Expansion Details And Why The Wildly Popular Skincare Brand Is Not Simply 'Clean,'" *Forbes*, September 3, 2019.

195 Ibid.

196 "Our Philosophy: The Drunk Elephant Difference," Drunk Elephant, accessed May 30, 2020.

197 Joanna Fu, "Drunk Elephant Founder Tiffany Masterson on Her 'Suspicious 6' Skincare Philosophy," *Vogue*, November 26, 2019.

The natural beauty movement calls for products that have minimal amounts of synthetic materials. Instead, these formulas contain ingredients sourced from nature, such as botanical oils, extracts, butters, and salts.[198] Drunk Elephant's website emphasizes that it does not take into account an ingredient's synthetic or natural status because many natural ingredients, such as essential oils, can cause skin reactions. The company instead focuses on soothing, low-hazard ingredients that are in no way questionable.[199]

To ensure that customers are aware of Drunk Elephant's stance on clean beauty, its website describes exactly what the company's items are formulated with and without. On each product's digital page, there are tabs that provide the colloquial name for the main ingredients alongside scientific information such as chemical compound names and pH levels. For example, the "Ingredients" tab for the T.L.C. Sukari Babyfacial explains that the face mask is made with chickpea flour, matcha tea, pumpkin ferment extract, and virgin marula oil, which are all easily understandable terms. Below these is the list of chemical terms associated with all of the ingredients.

Additionally, each product has a "Philosophy" tab that summarizes the decision to leave out the suspicious six. The tab also provides a link to a more informative "Philosophy" page, which discusses Drunk Elephant's clean-compatibility ethos

---

198 Rabia, "Beauty Education: The Difference Between Clean, Green, and Natural Beauty Products," Amaliah, March 15, 2019.

199 "Our Philosophy: The Drunk Elephant Difference," Drunk Elephant, accessed May 30, 2020.

in great detail and can be directly accessed from the website's main page.

Tiffany also chooses to remove ingredients that the public perceives negatively even though they have not been proven to be harmful. For example, she removed parabens, a class of popular preservatives, from her formulas simply because she wanted to put consumers' minds at ease.[200] A debate over the safety of parabens has divided beauty enthusiasts since a controversial study emerged in 2004 potentially linking them to cancer; since, many people have chosen to stop purchasing products containing them.[201] They are also banned in the European Union.[202] Although Tiffany does not believe that parabens in cosmetics are unsafe, she listened to customers' apprehension and found preservative alternatives.

The efforts of Drunk Elephant to quell any doubts about ingredient safety have helped to establish its reputation of trustworthiness. And the word on the street is that the products *work*.

From its inception, the company enjoyed massive popularity because its clean-compatible products deliver the results that people desire. According to fashion blogger Leandra Medine, one of Drunk Elephant's minority investors, the company was "one of the first clean brands that...[resonated] with a

---

200 Nicola Davis, "Is Clean Beauty a Skincare Revolution—or a Pointless Indulgence," *The Guardian*, February 4, 2019.

201 "By the Way, Doctor: Are Parabens Dangerous," Harvard Health Publishing: Harvard Medical School, March 2014.

202 Oliver Milman, "US Cosmetics Are Full of Chemicals Banned by Europe—Why," *The Guardian*, May 22, 2019.

customer who was not educated on clean skincare yet. There was so much conversation around the efficacy of the other clean brands, and that was never even a question with Drunk Elephant."[203]

Tiffany believes that using an exclusively Drunk Elephant regime is the best way to get maximum results. She claims, "a routine is only as good as its worst product, [and] a product only as good as its worst ingredient."[204] In interviews, she encourages people to try The Littles package, which contains a month's worth of eight travel-sized products that allow customers to test Tiffany's philosophy by taking a break from the suspicious six.[205]

Evidently, the company's approach is satisfying many. When speaking to *Vanity Fair* about modern consumers' tendency to eschew brand loyalty in favor of brand-hopping, Tiffany declared, "We've seen with Drunk Elephant that even though we have remarkably low awareness, we have healthy volume because we have a high retention rate."[206] In other words, even if not many people are aware of its existence, the company has a high volume of sales because its customers tend to return for repeat purchases.

---

203 Rachel Strugatz, "Why Shiseido Bought Drunk Elephant," *The Business of Fashion*, October 8, 2019.

204 Tiffany Masterson, "Founder Note," Drunk Elephant, accessed May 30, 2020.

205 Joanna Fu, "Drunk Elephant Founder Tiffany Masterson on Her 'Suspicious 6' Skincare Philosophy," *Vogue*, November 26, 2019.

206 Nora Maloney, "Drunk Elephant Founder Tiffany Masterson Takes Skincare by Storm," *Vanity Fair*, January 10, 2018.

Therein lies the key to its cult following: Drunk Elephant is able to meet the current demand among skincare enthusiasts for exceptional products with top-tier ingredients.

According to Priya Venkatesh, senior vice president of merchandising for skincare and hair at Sephora, Drunk Elephant is one of the fastest-growing skincare lines the retailer has ever sold.[207] Remarkably, this is true despite the very hefty price tag that accompanies all of Drunk Elephant's products. For instance, its popular vitamin C serum costs $80 for 30mL.

In its 2019 report, The NPD Group analyzed people's willingness to sacrifice affordability for ingredient assurance. Larissa Jensen, Vice President and Industry Advisor for the company's beauty sector, explained in the report that "the number of consumers who are making purchase decisions primarily based on the price of a product is decreasing" while "the significance of knowing exactly what they are putting on their skin becomes more important."[208]

Drunk Elephant has not only responded to this shift in buying habits with a clean-compatibility philosophy but it has also tailored its brand to young consumers. Its potent formulas, minimalist packaging, and quirky name have enabled the business to gain a loyal fanbase of Millennials and Generation Z.

---

[207] Rachel Strugatz, "Why Shiseido Bought Drunk Elephant," *The Business of Fashion*, October 8, 2019.

[208] "Empowered Consumers Want Clean Ingredients and Brand Transparency from Skincare Products," The NPD Group, August 14, 2019.

Its cult following elevated Drunk Elephant onto the skincare mainstream, spurring larger businesses to take notice. In 2019, Tiffany stunned the beauty entrepreneurship world when her company was acquired for $845 million by Shiseido, one of the oldest and largest cosmetics companies. The giant was rumored to have beaten Estée Lauder in the last round of bidding. *Forbes* declared that "the implied valuation [of $845 million] is more than eight times sales, making the Drunk Elephant acquisition one of the biggest ever for a skincare brand."[209]

Marc Rey, chief executive of Shiseido Americas and chief growth officer, revealed that "Drunk Elephant's approach to 'clean' beauty was an important consideration for us at Shiseido. As a global company, we are missing this very key market which we know is growing extremely rapidly and is not going to stop anytime soon."[210]

In a *Bloomberg* press release, Masahiko Uotani, president and CEO of Shiseido, went even further by asserting that Tiffany and the Drunk Elephant team will help Shiseido pursue its "long-term mission of 'Beauty Innovations for a Better World.'"[211] With this statement, he insinuated that Drunk Elephant's philosophy is improving the landscape of beauty; with publicly rigorous standards of ingredient safety, the company fosters a people-first culture that Shiseido wants to project.

---

209 Chloe Sorvino, "Hot Skin-Care Brand Drunk Elephant Sells For $845 Million, Minting Founder A Fortune," *Forbes*, October 8, 2019.

210 Rachel Strugatz, "Why Shiseido Bought Drunk Elephant," *The Business of Fashion*, October 8, 2019.

211 "Shiseido to Acquire Drunk Elephant," *Bloomberg*, October 7, 2019.

Entrepreneurs like Tiffany are especially well-poised to meet the market demand for clean makeup companies that emphasize a commitment to customers' skin. According to *The Business of Fashion*, legacy beauty brands owned by conglomerates are struggling to keep up: "To upend decades-old operations and processes to reformulate to meet clean standards on a global scale could be a multi-billion-dollar project."[212] Therefore, it is easier for giants like Shiseido, Estée Lauder, L'Oréal, Unilever, and Coty to purchase a clean indie venture and scale it.

The overall trend toward wellness in beauty has paved the way for indie companies like Drunk Elephant to build their brands off of easing the minds of hesitant customers. Since the FDA's regulatory actions are typically reactive to grave incidents of exposure to toxicity, it is up to companies to implement proactive measures that prioritize skin health.

In an industry bound by little oversight, beauty companies who can provide peace of mind to consumers become cult favorites.

---

212 Rachel Strugatz, "Why Shiseido Bought Drunk Elephant," *The Business of Fashion*, October 8, 2019.

CHAPTER 10

SELL ME AN EXPERIENCE

A slice of pink desert exists in the heart of West Hollywood. Young people swarm to the location on Melrose Place, phones in hand as they prepare to let all of Instagram know about this creation. When they enter through a pale blush door, they witness a retail version of an American Southwest landscape before them.

Textured walls resemble the sides of a canyon, and products sit atop exhibits that look like natural rock formations. Every surface and product in sight is the same shade of Millennial Pink, with dry grass and sun-washed plants offering golden pops of color. To evoke a road trip feel, rearview mirrors are placed beside product testers for customers to peer into as they experiment with formulas.

One room in the store houses a tall replica of Arizona's Antelope Canyon. It is complete with sounds recorded at the real site and day-to-night lighting that reflects the authentic color range of morning beige to sunset purple. A floor-to-ceiling mirror at one end of the replica enables customers to capture an ideal Instagram shot juxtaposing their city outfits with the curving rock formations.[213]

This store belongs to Glossier, a cosmetics and skincare company that has piqued enormous interest among young consumers and venture capitalists alike.

Emily Weiss, the founder of Glossier, started on her entrepreneurial path to unicorn status in 2010 with a beauty blog named *Into the Gloss*. At the time, she was an art school graduate working as a fashion assistant at *Vogue*. She conceived her blog for everyday women interested in insider beauty tips and interviews with designers, editors, and models. In one particularly popular segment called "Top Shelf," Emily's famous connections from *Vogue* allowed her to inquire about their go-to beauty habits and take photographs of the products in their bathroom cabinets. These photographs are known as "shelfies," a mix between "shelf" and "selfie." By 2012, the blog had more than 200 thousand monthly visitors.[214,215,216]

While running *Into the Gloss*, she realized that the blog's community of young women loved individual products but

---

[213] Hannah Huber, "The Top 5 Things We Want to Copy from Glossier's New L.A. Store," *Architectural Digest*, June 4, 2018.

[214] Kate Branch, "Emily Weiss on What a Glossier Girl Smells Like and Building a Cool Girl Empire," *Vogue*, September 15, 2017.

[215] Amy Larocca, "The Magic Skin of Glossier's Emily Weiss," *The Cut*, January 8, 2018.

[216] Marisa Meltzer, "How Emily Weiss's Glossier Grew From Millennial Catnip to Billion-Dollar Juggernaut," *Vanity Fair*, October 10, 2019.

were not deeply attached to any particular company.[217] Emily had a vision to launch a product-based extension of her blog that would achieve substantial consumer loyalty. Everything from the products' marketing to their designs to their formulations would be specifically crafted to appeal to Emily's Millennial audience.

She visited eleven venture capital firms, each of which rejected her. The twelfth firm, San Francisco-based Forerunner Ventures, embraced the vision. Its founder, Kirsten Green, helped Emily raise $2 million in seed funding the start the business.[218]

In October 2014, Glossier was born.

The company has experienced explosive growth, which is evident when considering its sequence of venture capital investments.

A month after Glossier launched its first four products, it received $8.4 million in Series A funding.[219] Series A funding is a step up from the initial seed funding, and its objective is to finance further team and product development. It is awarded when a company demonstrates that it has products

---

217 Kate Branch, "Emily Weiss on What a Glossier Girl Smells Like and Building a Cool Girl Empire," *Vogue*, September 15, 2017.

218 Marisa Meltzer, "How Emily Weiss's Glossier Grew From Millennial Catnip to Billion-Dollar Juggernaut," *Vanity Fair*, October 10, 2019.

219 Janna Mandell, "Glossier Just Got $52 Million In Fresh Capital, Bringing Total Funding To $86 Million," *Forbes*, February 22, 2018.

that satisfy early customers and provide feedback for future product development.[220]

In November 2016, Glossier raised $24 million in a Series B round, which is meant to elevate a business above the development stage and expand market reach beyond the initial customer base. It also permits quality talent acquisition, as evidenced by Glossier's 2017 acquisition of the Canadian technology agency Dynamo.[221] [222]

In February 2018, Glossier raised an additional $52 million in a Series C round, whose purpose is to rapidly and significantly scale a business with a history of growth.[223], [224] Within a year after the Series C round, Glossier's annual revenue more than doubled to surpass $100 million, it gained one million new customers, and it launched the Glossier Play brand to target those interested in bolder makeup looks.[225]

Finally, in March 2019, Glossier announced its newest funding success: $100 million in a Series D round that valued the company at $1.2 billion. By the end of 2019, Glossier had two

---

220 "Series A, B, C Funding: The Ultimate Guide," Fundz, accessed May 30, 2020.

221 Janna Mandell, "Glossier Just Got $52 Million In Fresh Capital, Bringing Total Funding To $86 Million," *Forbes*, February 22, 2018.

222 Nathan Reiff, "Series A, B, C Funding: How It Works," Investopedia, March 5, 2020.

223 Janna Mandell, "Glossier Just Got $52 Million In Fresh Capital, Bringing Total Funding To $86 Million," *Forbes*, February 22, 2018.

224 Nathan Reiff, "Series A, B, C Funding: How It Works," Investopedia, March 5, 2020.

225 Sarah Berger, "Glossier: How This 33-Year-Old Turned Her Beauty Blog to a $1 Billion Brand," *CNBC*, March 30, 2019.

permanent stores, numerous semi-permanent pop-ups, and 2.5 million Instagram followers.[226], [227]

How did Emily, a founder with zero business training, build a company that so intensely appeals to young consumers?

The answer lies in understanding how deeply young people prioritize experiences.

According to Euromonitor International's Lifestyles Survey of 2017, "about 45 percent of Millennials prefer to spend money on experiences, rather than things, compared to 39 percent of all respondents and 32 percent of Baby Boomers." The market research firm reported that this new emphasis on experiences "is causing established brands to experiment outside of their typical business models."[228]

However, as Emily told *Financial Times*, "It's really tough for any behemoth company to change channels and change direction. Look at how tied a lot of these companies are to offline channels and to ways of selling and…communicating with customers that are pre-social media. And then you look at a company like Glossier that was born on the Internet and born with the…promise of customer experience first and foremost."[229]

---

226 Ibid.

227 Jo Ellison, "Glossier's Emily Weiss: 'We're Creating the Estée Lauder of the Future,'" *Financial Times*, August 6, 2019.

228 Kayla Villena, "Millennial Beauty," Euromonitor International, January 23, 2019.

229 Jo Ellison, "Glossier's Emily Weiss: 'We're Creating the Estée Lauder of the Future,'" *Financial Times*, August 6, 2019.

Emily's secret to a successful business plan is an emphasis on creating customer-optimized experiences at every point of contact between customers and Glossier.

One of the most visible strategies of this experience-based focus is the company's product designs, which lend themselves to a very specific aesthetic.

At the beginning, the company launched with four products created to set the tone for the "Glossier Girl" archetype, which would come to define the Glossier brand. The all-purpose balm, facial mist, sheer skin tint, and moisturizer attracted a specific type of carefree, young consumer who desires a simple routine.

The Glossier Girl embodies the spirit of ease and effortless glamour. She pounces the company's sheer face tint onto her skin with her fingers, blots some Cloud Paint gel-cream blush on her cheeks, swipes a transparent lip gloss on, brushes Boy Brow gel through her thick eyebrows, and is out the door. As *Document Journal* elucidated, "The Glossier Girl is carefree, charming, and preternaturally beautiful…Her coy smile suggests that with the right combination of product and lifestyle, we too could attain this state of perfect imperfection."[230]

A critical aspect of the Glossier Girl archetype is a skincare routine that transforms the face into a smooth canvas ready for Glossier's sheer makeup products. The company provides

---

[230] Camille Sojit, "Glossier, #NoMakeup, and the Authenticity Myth," *Document Journal*, November 4, 2019.

an array of skincare options that meet this need and further emphasize its mission of building a naturally beautiful face.

According to Kayla Marci, market analyst at retail data firm Edited, "With brands like Glossier and Drunk Elephant seeing success in the market, there has been a noticeable shift in beauty from cosmetics into skincare. Trends like heavy contouring have fallen out of favor as consumers take a more natural approach to their skin, focusing on getting the base clean and healthy."[231]

When I interviewed Daana Bajnauth, a Georgetown University economics major, about the future of the beauty industry, she spoke of the trend toward natural techniques: "I think that makeup is becoming less about a complete transformation and more about enhancing one's features. People are taking care of their skin underneath the makeup and deciding that they no longer need thick layers of products to conceal everything. A little tinted moisturizer, although sheer, can go a long way in improving someone's confidence."

Glossier has both driven and profited off of this shift in mentality. Its "Skin First, Makeup Second" marketing approach is reflected not only in its status as both a makeup and skincare company but also in its formulas. There are no drastic before-and-after comparisons that emerge from using Glossier. Rather than showcase an extraordinary final result, the products celebrate the *experience* of becoming an effortless Glossier Girl with a few ritualistic steps.

---

231 Hayley Peterson, "VSCO Girls Are Upending the Cosmetics Industry by Eschewing Makeup in Favor of Facial Sprays and Creams," *Business Insider*, October 23, 2019.

Although the company was conceived for *Into the Gloss*'s Millennial audience, its minimalistic yet polished look is very popular among Generation Z teenagers who identify with the "VSCO girl" subculture. This subculture has its name from the photography app VSCO, and it refers to a teen who embraces casual, natural beauty and laidback fashion trends. Articles written about this type of girl frequently mention Glossier as a staple company that caters to this aesthetic.[232]

It is undeniable that Glossier's complexion products are for people who do not struggle with serious skin problems. Their lightweight formulas are not made to conceal discoloration, acne, age spots, or enlarged pores. While some critics argue that the products are crafted for traditionally beautiful people and therefore reinforce the unrealistic ideal of a flawless face, supporters assert that they encourage people to embrace the natural state of their skin.[233]

Certainly, the washes of color that the products provide cannot do much in the way of a *physical* transformation. They are best suited to those seeking a *mental* confidence-boost created by a nonchalant approach to makeup. Ease of application is fundamental to this experience. Glossier Girls do not need to work products; instead, products work for them.

Another means of creating experiences for its customers is through marketing techniques that aim to build a community.

---

[232] Ibid.

[233] Camille Sojit, "Glossier, #NoMakeup, and the Authenticity Myth," *Document Journal*, November 4, 2019.

Unlike Kylie Jenner, Emily is purposefully not at the forefront of her brand. As *Vanity Fair*'s Marisa Meltzer wrote after meeting with her, "The surprise in tagging along with [Emily] to the flagship [store in Manhattan] isn't the fanfare—it's the lack...Most people seem not so much to politely leave her alone as to have no idea who she is. [Emily] takes that as a very good sign, surveying the room and smiling at her anonymity: 'It's more than me.'"[234]

Glossier Girls are reflections of a certain "look" rather than of a specific individual. A glance through Glossier's Instagram and YouTube content illustrates the diversity of people who can embody this effortlessly chic look. Rather than spend thousands of dollars on beautifully photographed celebrities, Glossier posts pictures and videos from Glossier employees and small Instagram influencers of different races, ages, and genders. Their faces do not appear to have been edited, and they showcase the products in selfie shots that do not look like obvious advertisements. To drive the point home, the company's slogan is "Beauty Inspired by Real Life."

Another method of creating community through marketing is peer referrals. Glossier has been offering a peer referral program for years. Any registered Glossier customer can send out a unique link to friends and family, and if anybody makes a purchase using that link, the registered customer will then earn a discount worth up to $10.[235] The practice is similar to the commission that influencers make when

---

234 Marisa Meltzer, "How Emily Weiss's Glossier Grew From Millennial Catnip to Billion-Dollar Juggernaut," *Vanity Fair*, October 10, 2019.
235 "Referral Program Terms & Conditions," Glossier, accessed May 30, 2020.

people purchase products using their affiliate links. The critical difference, however, is that this program establishes a kind of marketing that appears much more "real" than advertisements or influencer promotions; when customers encourage their own friends and families to purchase from Glossier, the referral is personal.

In return, the discount to registered customers is a kind of reward that honors their loyalty to the company. This motivates them not only to keep returning to Glossier, but also to continue to share their positive experiences with others. Unsurprisingly, around 70 percent of the company's online sales and traffic are driven through peer-to-peer referral.[236]

As *The Fader* noted, Emily is building "a new version of the friend-centric economy best exemplified by Avon: young women rely on a circle of friends as focus groups whose insights and retweets can help them sell their products, brands, and ideologies directly to their peers." This mode of encouraging existing customers to convince their friends to purchase from Glossier is "a technologically sophisticated update to…Avon Ladies: rather than go door-to-door, [Emily] goes screen-to-screen."[237]

In addition to products and marketing, Glossier's status as a "Direct-to-Consumer" (D2C) business is the bedrock of the company's experience-based specialization.

---

[236] *Recode*, "Glossier CEO Emily Weiss | Full Interview | 2018 Code Commerce," September 18, 2018, video, 31:10.

[237] Haley Mlotek, "How Glossier Harnessed The Myth Of Cool Girl Makeup," *The Fader*, August 17, 2016.

D2C refers to a company's sale of a product directly to consumers without intermediaries like big department stores. Glossier chose this route before D2C was mainstream, becoming one of the first indie companies to achieve hyper customer-centricity.

Before starting her business, Emily "noticed that the beauty conglomerates had a top-down way of communicating—via celebrity ads or department store placements." She knew from her blog's comments that her target demographic preferred a more conversational relationship, and she ensured that Glossier would provide it.[238]

As a D2C business, Glossier can rapidly respond to customers on every platform, control purchasing experiences online and in-store, and construct a pipeline of customer feedback. This feedback reaches not only customer service employees, but also the marketing, development, and product teams; everybody is kept in the loop on the subject of customer satisfaction.[239]

In fact, Emily mentioned this organizational structure in a YouTube interview with Goldman Sachs, which has received over 150 thousand views. She shared that Glossier's "customer support team is in our marketing team. It is not in a dark

---

238 Marisa Meltzer, "How Emily Weiss's Glossier Grew From Millennial Catnip to Billion-Dollar Juggernaut," *Vanity Fair*, October 10, 2019.

239 Inge Lammertink, "Why Glossier Embodies the Future of Shopping and B2C Marketing," Medium, February 11, 2019.

corner in a different office. [It is] one of the strongest, most incredible teams in our company."[240]

Following the tradition of *Into the Gloss*, Emily ensured that fans would feel heard. After all, she views consumers as a prime source of research and development, and their critiques enable the company to improve. Glossier's marketing, editorial, and customer service teams respond to Instagram questions publicly or through direct message, and the company builds mini focus groups on the platform.[241]

For instance, in 2015, Emily asked readers to leave comments on *Into the Gloss* detailing the characteristics that their dream face cleanser would have. Using the feedback, Glossier released Milky Jelly Cleanser the following year. When it asked followers for help once again in creating a perfect moisturizer, the responses guided the company in creating its Priming Moisturizer Rich.[242] The philosophy behind this practice is perfectly encapsulated in Glossier's "About Us" page, which states, "We're building the future beauty company where everything we make starts with you. We create the products you tell us you wish existed."[243]

To sustain this massive online D2C presence, Glossier has prioritized investments in digital tools. Much of the

---

[240] *Goldman Sachs*, "Emily Weiss: Rethinking the Business of Beauty," January 18, 2019, video, 20:44.

[241] Alyssa Giacobbe, "How Glossier Hacked Social Media to Build A Cult-Like Following," *Entrepreneur*, August 15, 2017.

[242] Haley Mlotek, "How Glossier Harnessed The Myth Of Cool Girl Makeup," *The Fader*, August 17, 2016.

[243] "About," Glossier, accessed May 30, 2020.

venture capital funding raised has gone to "doubling down on platforms, doubling down on glossier.com and, in doing so, enabling customers to continue to be advocates for the brand."[244]

In a YouTube interview with *Recode*, Emily revealed, "We see ourselves very much as a tech company whose business is beauty products...We create products in conjunction with our global community. What we're looking to do is basically bring that community home" by building the best digital environment for members to share stories of how Glossier products worked for them.[245] This objective explains Glossier's purchase of technology agency Dynamo; as a result of the acquisition, one-third of Glossier's total workforce of two hundred employees are in technology.[246]

By operating as a D2C business, Glossier has devised a consumer-up approach that is distinct from most companies' brand-down framework. At its core, this approach ensures that all of its employees are working to not only create the most pleasurable digital experience for its customers but also to foster a sense that the company is continually listening to fans.

The final component of the Glossier experience is the ability to produce digital content with the company's branding.

---

244 *Recode*, "Glossier CEO Emily Weiss | Full Interview | 2018 Code Commerce," September 18, 2018, video, 31:10.

245 Ibid.

246 Inge Lammertink, "Why Glossier Embodies the Future of Shopping and B2C Marketing," Medium, February 11, 2019.

The minimalistic packaging colored in shades of pink, white, and black practically lends itself to social media posts, which explains why most of the pictures on the Glossier Instagram are of zoomed-in products. The company's Millennial Pink hoodie, which has "Glossier" stamped in white lettering across the front, achieves the same goal. Emily decided from the beginning of Glossier's launch that she wanted to create a company whose sweatshirts people would want to show off in public.[247]

The most obvious example of Glossier's emphasis on being "Instagrammable" is its retail locations. In addition to the Los Angeles store, which features the American Southwest desert theme, the first version of the Manhattan store was an early indicator that Glossier's experience-based retail concept struck gold. This original showroom, built in 2017, was decorated to look like a luxury bathroom that encouraged consumers to mill around and test products in front of giant mirrors. With its visuals and opportunities for tactile testing, it followed Apple's model of multi-sensory stimulation.[248] Inge Lammertink from *Medium* remarked when entering the Manhattan showroom, "It was like entering an Apple store for Beauty."[249]

---

247 Amy Larocca, "The Magic Skin of Glossier's Emily Weiss," *The Cut*, January 8, 2018.

248 Carmine Gallo, "Apple Retail Stores and the 'Buying Brain,'" *Entrepreneur*, April 24, 2012.

249 Inge Lammertink, "Why Glossier Embodies the Future of Shopping and B2C Marketing," Medium, February 11, 2019.

It was also lucrative. According to *Forbes*, it generated more revenue per square foot than the average Apple store.[250] In fact, Inge noted that her friends had warned her about the long line of people who were usually waiting outside the entrance.

The official New York flagship store that replaced the showroom in November 2018 follows a similar design. It features large mirrors, red couches, and counters of products, which make the space feel like a beauty room in a mansion. There is a separate room for testing items, which is decorated like a bathroom with slate sinks and mirrored shelves of Glossier products lining the walls. Much like the Los Angeles location's "Antelope Canyon," the Manhattan store has a section dedicated to taking pictures: a room housing human-sized replicas of Boy Brow eyebrow gel. There are no cash registers in sight to mar the vibe; instead, sales associates clad in pink jumpsuits walk around with iPads to complete transactions.

Even the entrance lends itself to being on a Snapchat story. Customers walk up red, carpeted stairs surrounded by a pink plaster wall that curves into a tall cylinder around a skylight. According to the architectural firm that oversaw the space renovation, "the idea was to kind of make a stairway to heaven."[251]

Every detail of Glossier fortifies its message that customer experience is first and foremost. Its products, social media

---

250 Chris Walton, "Glossier To Open New Flagship Store In New York," *Forbes*, November 5, 2018.
251 Richard Lawson, "Online Makeup Startup Invites Customers Inside With a 'Stairway to Heaven,'" LoopNet, March 26, 2019.

marketing, D2C status, and photogenic branding culminate into a business model that has fascinated consumers and venture capitalists alike. Without any business background, Emily has built a unicorn company that taps into the exciting side of shopping experiences.

Her approach strikes such a chord with Generation Z and Millennial consumers that she was included in the 2019 list of *Time*'s "100 Next," which spotlights one hundred rising stars who are shaping their industries.

Alexis Ohanian, co-founder of Reddit and husband to Serena Williams, wrote a profile of Emily for *Time* after she was announced as one of the "100 Next" stars.[252] He affirmed, "From reinventing the makeup counter to canonizing the #shelfie, Emily has helped a generation of consumers feel good about themselves—something the beauty industry has historically failed to do."

---

252 Alexis Ohanian, "Emily Weiss," *Time*, accessed May 30, 2020.

CHAPTER 11

CLASS IS IN SESSION

What do mathematics and eyebrows have in common?

While some would argue that there is no connection between the two, Anastasia Soare would beg to differ. Known as the "Eyebrow Queen," she is the creator of the patented Golden Ratio Eyebrow Shaping Method. This technique has catapulted her to the helm of a multi-billion-dollar business.

Born in Constanța, Romania, to parents who were tailors, Anastasia has always been fixated on proportionality. She majored in art history and architecture in college, where she studied the golden ratio that renders figures most pleasing to the eye.[253] This ratio of two quantities, defined by Greek mathematician Euclid and named "phi" after the Greek sculptor Phidias, is approximately equal to 1.618:1. An example of a rectangle that adheres to this ratio has sides with a length of 1.618 units and a width of one unit. Phi has appeared in geometry, architecture, and art throughout human civilization,

---

253 Alyssa Reeder and Anastasia Soare, "Anastasia Soare Of Anastasia Beverly Hills Shares Her Beauty Routine," *Into The Gloss*, May 19, 2015.

and many scholars argue that it has been used in works such as Egypt's Pyramids of Giza, Greece's Parthenon, and some of Leonardo Da Vinci's drawings.[254]

In her art history classes, Anastasia also learned the importance of eyebrows when creating faces. As she shared in an interview with *LA Times*, one of her professors "believed that if you draw a portrait and want to change an emotion, you change the eyebrow shape." He taught her about "Leonardo da Vinci's theory that the body is in great proportion" and about guidelines like the golden ratio that determine what features to draw on different face structures to make them most appealing.[255]

It was not until more than a decade later than Anastasia channeled this knowledge into a business, founding Anastasia Beverly Hills with the objective of introducing a new cosmetic vision to the beauty industry. She decided to build a venture that would not only provide professional-grade products, but that would also make them accessible to the average consumer through education.

Anastasia's story of entrepreneurship began when she arrived in Los Angeles, fleeing the brutal communist regime of Nicolae Ceaușescu. Her husband, a Romanian naval captain, had asked for political asylum at the United States Embassy while docked in Italy in 1987. Anastasia and their daughter Norvina

---

254 Gary Meisner, "Phi and the Golden Section in Architecture," The Golden Number, March 5, 2013.

255 Ingrid Schmidt, "Eyebrow Guru Anastasia Soare's 'A-Ha!' Moment? It Was Inspired by Da Vinci. Now, 'She Creates a Masterpiece,'" *Los Angeles Times*, December 14, 2017.

joined him in the United States two years later, a mere few months before a revolution ignited in Romania.[256]

As an immigrant who could not speak English, Anastasia found a job as an esthetician in a salon. She had taken cosmetology classes in Romania before defecting because she knew this field would not require advanced language skills.[257] While working at the salon, she realized that Americans were not paying much attention to eyebrows. While Romanian estheticians customarily tweezed brows before facials, Anastasia's boss refused to offer this service to clients.[258]

In response, Anastasia decided to rent a room at another salon and start her own small business dedicated to shaping brows. As she told *Into The Gloss*, "Everybody thought I was out of my mind. Number one, I don't speak the language. Number two, there are people who are born in this country that don't have their own businesses, and here I try to open my own business. 'I don't care,' I told myself. 'I have to do it.' I came here to be relevant, to be significant, and I wanted to do more than I did in Romania."[259]

She crafted her golden ratio method, which dictates that "brows should begin directly above the middle of your nostrils. The highest point of the arch should connect the tip

---

256 Lisa Boren, "Soare," *Los Angeles Business Journal*, July 19, 1999.
257 *Beautylish*, "The History of Anastasia Beverly Hills," August 4, 2013, video, 4:20.
258 Jessica Prince Erlich, "How I Get It Done: Beauty Entrepreneur Anastasia Soare," *The Cut*, January 2, 2018.
259 Alyssa Reeder and Anastasia Soare, "Anastasia Soare Of Anastasia Beverly Hills Shares Her Beauty Routine," *Into The Gloss*, May 19, 2015.

of the nose with the middle of the iris. Brows should end where the corner of the nostril connects with the outer corner of the eye."[260] According to Anastasia, this approach produces eyebrows that are optimally proportional for every bone structure. Influenced by a classical background in art history and architecture, she believes that this kind of facial balance is the foundation of beauty.

Her philosophy resonated with models like Cindy Crawford and Naomi Campbell, who helped to spread the word about Anastasia's skills. She even appeared live on *The Oprah Winfrey Show*, launching her technique "into the forefront of the national consciousness," as her website asserts. In 1997, she opened a salon in Beverly Hills that attracted celebrity clientele.[261]

When actress Poppy Montgomery, one of Anastasia's clients, was cast to star in a movie filmed in Canada, she was concerned that the makeup artist on set would not know how to maintain her eyebrow shape. As Anastasia recounted in an interview with *Harper's Bazaar*, she responded to Poppy by saying, "Let me go to the art store and find a sheet of plastic. I will cut us a form." In addition to this stencil, she mixed some Vaseline with aloe vera and powder to create a colored wax. Poppy used this kit while filming, and when she returned five months later, she encouraged Anastasia to turn it into a commercial product.[262]

---

260 "About Anastasia Beverly Hills," Anastasia Beverly Hills, accessed May 30, 2020.

261 "A Visual Timeline," Anastasia Beverly Hills, accessed May 30, 2020.

262 *Harper's Bazaar*, "Eyebrow Queen Anastasia Soare Shows off Her Insane Beauty Collection," June 28, 2019, video, 10:43.

In 2000, Anastasia Beverly Hills released a brow shaping kit based on its founder's patented method, thereby filling the eyebrow market niche in the United States.[263] Armed with instructions, tools, and an array of stencils as guidance, all makeup lovers would be able to learn how to create the perfect arch to frame their faces.

Still, there was work to be done on the information front. Eyebrows in the 1990s and early 2000s were over-plucked and overpowered by other features, and consumers were not accustomed to Anastasia's kit. When Nordstrom began to sell the item, she visited its department stores every weekend to show clients how to use the stencils, wax, powders, and brushes in the kit.[264] As Anastasia told *The Cut*, "I needed about ten years to convince everyone around the country that eyebrows are important."[265]

Two decades later, Anastasia Beverly Hills is worth over $3 billion and has flourished in the face of shifting consumer norms.[266] It commands widespread respect throughout the beauty community, rivaling much newer ventures in its capacity to entice Generation Z and Millennials.

At its core, the company has preserved its original objective of elevating the industry through high-quality products and education.

---

263 "A Visual Timeline," Anastasia Beverly Hills, accessed May 30, 2020.
264 Ibid.
265 Jessica Prince Erlich, "How I Get It Done: Beauty Entrepreneur Anastasia Soare," *The Cut*, January 2, 2018.
266 "Anastasia Soare," *Forbes*, June 3, 2019.

On its website's "About" page, Anastasia Beverly Hills describes itself as a business that "creates prestige cosmetics for a passionate prosumer audience."[267] The kind of "prosumer" that Anastasia targets is an amateur consumer who purchases professional products. Prosumers have emerged en masse in response to social media influencers pulling back the curtain of secrecy in the beauty industry. These influencers divulge their makeup secrets on every platform, empowering viewers to elevate their own artistic skills. As a result, Generation Z and Millennial beauty enthusiasts expect expert-grade products that deliver immediate payoff and generate impactful looks that mimic those on their screens.

However, Anastasia Beverly Hills goes a step further in harnessing this type of prosumer. Rather than leave product education solely up to influencers, Anastasia channels her past of instruction into her business. She originally helped to ignite a "brow revolution" through a two-pronged approach of teaching the golden ratio while introducing products that accompany the technique.[268] Anastasia took up the mantle of "Professor of Makeup" in the decades before makeup education was accessible to the public. She was doing the work of the modern beauty community before anybody could even conceptualize how social media would change consumer habits.

In the current age, Anastasia turns consumers into prosumers by providing expert tools alongside extensive information

---

267 "About Anastasia Beverly Hills," Anastasia Beverly Hills, accessed May 30, 2020.
268 Ibid.

that amplifies the lessons of beauty influencers. Formed by its founder's legacy of guiding customers in the direction of product optimization, Anastasia Beverly Hills is a powerhouse of professional cosmetics that appeal to the masses.

Education is still baked into the DNA of the company, in part because its comprehensive ranges may overwhelm even experienced makeup lovers. For eyebrows alone, it sells primers, stencils, pomades, three types of pencils, powders, highlighting crayons, gels, and various brushes. The company also offers six highlighter kits and four contour kits, each bearing either four or six shades, in addition to individual highlighter and bronzer compacts in various hues. With these diverse options, it is helpful for customers to learn from experts how to perfectly select, apply, and layer products.

The company provides a bulk of its guidance through its Instagram account, which enjoys an impressive following of more than twenty million people. Norvina, Anastasia's daughter, viewed Instagram as a gold mine from its early days. She started the Anastasia Beverly Hills account in 2013 to communicate with consumers about how to use the company's products.[269] Instead of traveling to department stores to connect with two hundred women who wanted to learn about eyebrows, contour, and eyeshadow, Anastasia began to reach thousands of people daily with images and tutorials. These followers were just starting to form a beauty community based upon experimentation and shared knowledge.

---

269 Jessica Prince Erlich, "How I Get It Done: Beauty Entrepreneur Anastasia Soare," *The Cut*, January 2, 2018.

As a testament to Instagram's significance, Anastasia revealed in an interview with *The Cut* that the platform is behind the success of one of the company's bestselling products, a colored eyebrow wax called the Dipbrow pomade. She originally released the item in 2000, but "it was so advanced that no one wanted it. So we had to pull it." She relaunched it after joining Instagram because the platform made it "a lot easier to teach the client. At the beginning, no one liked it because they would dip so much and it looked so heavy [on the eyebrows]. Well, with education, they learned, and now everyone cannot live without Dipbrow."[270]

In fact, Dipbrow fueled the "Instagram brow" trend, which took root shortly after the product was released. This kind of eyebrow is bold and defined, a look that is created by laying down pomade as a base before powder and gel. By releasing the product that popularized this technique, Anastasia molded the beauty culture on Instagram from the platform's early years.

There is a kind of subdued elegance that has always defined Anastasia's presence on Instagram. Her company's page is polished, professional, and curated for artistry-driven viewers. It serves as a public portfolio of her items' potential. Unlike Huda Beauty's page, it very rarely features memes, humorous fads, and images of its founder and her family. Instead, it emphasizes practical application and technique. The account mainly reposts influencers' images, which serve as a source of inspiration for creating an array of makeup looks, and their tutorials, which walk through the steps

---

270 Ibid.

required to achieve beautiful end results with the company's products. The account also features Anastasia Beverly Hills makeup artists who share their step-by-step process of sculpting a particular feature.

With a focus on weaving instructional clips among product promotion, the page is as close to academic as companies can be on the platform. Despite the lack of clickbait posts and viral hacks, the approach resonates with more than twenty million followers—an amount that has enabled Anastasia Beverly Hills to be ranked among the most followed beauty companies on the platform.[271]

The company's website also embodies the mission of arming consumers with artistry knowledge. It accomplishes this through two features that are impossible to miss: the main page's "Explore" and "How To" tabs, which are positioned right next to the "Products" button that customers use to shop.

The "Explore" tab encourages customers to envision what they can achieve by purchasing from Anastasia Beverly Hills. It links to a page that features scores of Instagram influencers organized by the types of products that they are wearing. The categories cover eyebrows, eyes, face, lips, and body, thereby encompassing much of what the company sells. By providing completed looks from influencers with various preferences, ranging from subtle neutrals to vivid neons, these images

---

271 J. Clement, "Instagram: Most-Followed Beauty Brands 2019," Statista, December 3, 2019.

help customers visualize the diversity of styles to which Anastasia Beverly Hills items can adapt.

On the other hand, the "How To" tab is a video hub. It directs customers to a page housing a series of tutorials that feature makeup artists or Anastasia herself demonstrating application methods on models. These videos are also linked on each corresponding item's product page, ensuring that customers will see them. By publishing these instructional tutorials in a visible and centralized place, Anastasia Beverly Hills accentuates its message that expansive ranges of highly pigmented makeup do not have to be intimidating.

This idea is the epitome of today's beauty community, comprised of curious Generation Z and Millennial enthusiasts who seek guidance in their exploration of color. Anastasia Beverly Hills may not be alone in offering high-quality products, collaborating with influencers, and skillfully maneuvering social media, but it *is* unique in its prioritization of education.

Built upon a foundation of its founder's own scholarship and her past of training others, Anastasia Beverly Hills meets both the tangible and intangible needs of prosumers. With expansive ranges of tools and avenues of sharing knowledge, the company enables customers to fulfill their makeup aspirations. The underlying message is inspirational: what you dream, you can create. After all, as Anastasia shared in an interview with *Fashion Magazine,* "knowledge is power."[272]

---

272 Souzan Michael, "Anastasia Soare (of Anastasia Beverly Hills) Told Us The Secrets to Her Brand's Massive Success," *Fashion Magazine*, October 15, 2018.

In an oversaturated market in which every business labors to release the perfect item and campaign for customers, a company that offers resources and advice alongside its products and marketing emerges as reputable. It is essential in today's industry to offer something *more*, and Anastasia Beverly Hills achieves this by rendering professional glamour accessible to all.

Anastasia discovered her American dream in teaching people how to enhance their faces according to a venerated ratio, and by honoring and amplifying this legacy, her business integrates itself into the fabric of the inquisitive beauty community.

CHAPTER 12

EMBRACING DIVERGENCE

What comes to mind when you think about the outer packaging of makeup products?

Do images of generic black compacts and lipstick bullets come to mind? Do you think of nondescript plastic tubes and glass bottles that are not associated with a particular company? Are the containers sleek, minimalist, and glossy?

When Cashmere Nicole contemplated this question, she had an entirely different vision: egg-shaped blending sponges nestled in cardboard egg cartons, setting powders enveloped in paper flour bags, eyeliners encased in containers shaped like lollipops, loose highlighters housed in small ice cream tubs. She built a company, aptly named Beauty Bakerie, that is immediately recognizable across social media by its baking imagery.

Beauty companies typically do not feature such strong overtones of a specific theme in every product that they launch. Beauty Bakerie, however, intentionally diverges from this standard. Every shade, product name, and piece of packaging evokes the imagery of baked goods and sweets, enabling Cashmere to differentiate her business from its competitors. In fact, this aesthetic is so fundamental to the company's branding that Huda Beauty was accused of copying from Beauty Bakerie when it released a collection of setting powders accompanied by a baking-themed promotional campaign.

Beauty Bakerie's quirky packaging is especially important because the company has been based online for much of its existence. Unable to feel textures or test products through their screens, customers are instead hooked by the eye-catching baking motif that does not usually appear in cosmetic advertising. Although Beauty Bakerie has since expanded into Ulta Beauty, Boots, and Morphe brick-and-mortars, the company still predominantly advertises on social media and must contend with the over-saturation of online makeup content.[273] When fighting for the attention of young consumers who swipe without pause through endless images of products, peculiar packaging is invaluable.

According to Alexis DeSalva, retail and e-commerce senior analyst at market research firm Mintel, "about a quarter of online beauty shoppers aged eighteen to thirty-four added a beauty product to their cart because the packaging looked

---

273 Shammara Lawrence, "The Beauty Brands to Know Helmed by Black Women," Medium, February 17, 2020.

unique or exciting."²⁷⁴ Cashmere crafted a company that targets these kinds of young consumers that Alex mentioned. Given that the vast majority of her customers are exactly in this eighteen to thirty-four age range, her strategy of creating visual intrigue is perfectly suited to her target demographic.²⁷⁵

Many young consumers have been introduced to Beauty Bakerie through YouTube influencers, who are all eager to showcase something fun and exciting to their subscribers. For example, in a video that received over one million views, Tati Westbrook shared her first impression of the company. She declared, "Of all the indie brands, I really love how cute the packaging is," specifying that the theme of bakery goods persuaded her to experiment with Beauty Bakerie's products.²⁷⁶

Tati's comment gives insight into how important it is for beauty companies to bring something different to the table. Since influencers are continuously bombarded by launches and endless shipments of free makeup from companies, they are predisposed to notice brands that stand out from the generic sea of products. With an innovative theme, Beauty Bakerie injects a breath of fresh air into the industry and quickly catches their attention.

---

274 Cheryl Wischhover, "3 Founders on How to Build a Modern Beauty Brand," *Vogue Business*, June 16, 2019.

275 Amy Feldman, "How A Single Mom Battling Breast Cancer Built Beauty Bakerie To A $5M Brand, Got Unilever To Invest," *Forbes*, December 3, 2017.

276 *Tati*, "Beauty Bakerie | Hot or Not," June 15, 2017, video, 13:36.

YouTuber KathleenLights confirmed this sentiment in a video that received more than 700 thousand views: "I love everything about this brand. They're so unique, so creative." To emphasize the point, she showed a Beauty Bakerie eyeshadow palette decorated with pictures of Graham crackers surrounding the phrase, "Do it for the Graham."[277] This cleverly echoes the popular saying "Do it for the gram," which refers to an action done solely for the purpose of posting it on Instagram.

With this kind of thematic messaging, Beauty Bakerie upholds the idea that makeup at its core is a form of artistic expression. By housing its products in an exterior that is itself a form of art, the company engenders excitement before the consumer even opens her palette.

Another way in which Beauty Bakerie has diverged from the industry norm is through its founder's willingness to be vulnerable with her supporters about personal struggles and triumphs. Rather than glossing over her hardships or remaining a behind-the-scenes CEO, Cashmere intentionally weaves her story of perseverance into the branding of Beauty Bakerie.

The "About" page of the company's website is a letter from Cashmere detailing her life's ups and downs and featuring a photograph of her and her daughter. She also shares her history in interviews and on her personal Instagram account, which is linked in the bio of the company's account.

---

277 *KathleenLights*, "Full Face Beauty Bakerie | First Impressions," August 8, 2018, video, 18:20.

Cashmere's story of entrepreneurship began when she was a child. As she reminisced on her website, "Every Saturday I would beg my mom to take me to the library and I'd leave with at least ten books on how to start a business, writ[e] business plans, and anything relating to business. I remember watching Nickelodeon and hearing them say, 'We are coming right back with so and so and she's going to tell us how she began her brand.' I would run to fill my bowl of cereal during the quick break and make a mad dash back to the television with my notepad in hand."[278]

However, she became pregnant at the age of sixteen and needed to redirect her energy to support her daughter. She worked multiple jobs and relied on food stamps while finishing high school and college. In *Glamour*, Cashmere recalled, "I lived in this survival mode. As a single mom, you don't really have a choice. If you don't keep going, if you stop today, it's a matter of if you eat or not."[279]

Eventually, she put herself through nursing school and saved enough money to start Beauty Bakerie in 2011.[280] Cashmere elucidated the origin of the name in an interview with *Paper*, stating that the company has "a three-pronged approach: my love of the arts, my love for pastries…and my love of giving back and helping other people…I think the name 'Beauty Bakerie' and this idea of the sweet life is a combination of

---

278 "Our Story," Beauty Bakerie, accessed May 30, 2020.

279 Bella Cacciatore, "Cashmere Nicole Is What a 2019 CEO Looks Like," *Glamour*, August 13, 2019.

280 Amy Feldman, "How A Single Mom Battling Breast Cancer Built Beauty Bakerie To A $5M Brand, Got Unilever To Invest," *Forbes*, December 3, 2017.

those three things. It's a multifaceted approach to taking care of all parts of the person and beautifying all parts of the person."[281]

Finally, Cashmere was in a position to follow her dream. She launched a company that was not only creative, but that would also give a portion of its profit to charity. Through its Sugar Homes program, it has donated over $110,000 to two orphanages in Uganda.[282]

Unfortunately, another hurdle appeared shortly after the company's inception: Cashmere discovered a lump in her breast and was eventually diagnosed with intermediate breast cancer.[283]

Her diagnosis forced her to halt all business operations as she recovered from a double mastectomy. When she was ready to resume in the middle of 2013, she created a fundraiser titled Broken Boobs on the crowdfunding website IndieGoGo. Its objective was to aid her in relaunching Beauty Bakerie. Although she only received $570 of her $25,000 goal, the fundraiser caught the eye of Beyoncé, who featured Cashmere on her website for Breast Cancer Awareness month in 2014.[284]

---

[281] Ethan D'Spain, "Beauty Bakerie's Cashmere Nicole Is Better, Not Bitter," *Paper*, December 4, 2018.

[282] "Sugar Homes," Beauty Bakerie, accessed May 30, 2020.

[283] Victoria Uwumarogie, "Cashmere Nicole Put Off Seeing A Doctor About The Lump In Her Breast Until It Was Too Big Too Ignore—And Cancerous," *MadameNoire*, October 29, 2019.

[284] Bella Cacciatore, "Cashmere Nicole Is What a 2019 CEO Looks Like," *Glamour*, August 13, 2019.

This boost in morale and audience reach encouraged Cashmere to continue to fight for her dream. As she expressed to *Refinery29*, "I was so physically exhausted due to my medical issues. All of my money and tax returns went into building a website, planning photoshoots…plus I had a daughter to raise all by myself! At one point I seriously considered deleting the website and completely giving up, but…I didn't want cancer to win and I knew my idea had potential."[285]

Cashmere began to advertise through sponsored Instagram posts of models rubbing their lips and arms to show that swatches of the company's Lip Whip Liquid Lipstick did not smudge.[286] One of the ads went viral, prompting *Allure* to write that Lip Whips are the cockroach of lipsticks because they "could probably outlast an apocalypse."[287]

Beauty Bakerie's big break had arrived.

Cashmere recognizes the power of her history. When reflecting on the qualities that make her company stand out, she remarked, "I think our formulas and packaging pique the curiosity of the customer, but it seems to be my life story of trials and triumph that really intrigues them. How I went from nothing to something gives everyone hope…it's comforting when I look in hindsight and consider that this was

---

285 Aimee Simeon, "How Breast Cancer & Beyoncé Fueled This Beauty Mogul's Appetite For Success," *Refinery29*, November 6, 2018.
286 Bella Cacciatore, "Cashmere Nicole Is What a 2019 CEO Looks Like," *Glamour*, August 13, 2019.
287 Devon Abelman, "Beauty Bakerie Lip Whip Will Not Budge for Anything," *Allure*, November 11, 2016.

the reason I even had to endure so much—to lead others and show them that they can overcome challenges."[288]

YouTube influencer Jackie Aina echoed this notion in her video, "Full Face of Women-Owned Beauty Brands," which received over 800 thousand views: "I just can't even imagine going through all of the things that I go through as a woman on top of having a life-threatening illness...I look to her not only as an amazing brand, but as a role model."[289]

Some studies of young consumers' preferences confirm the importance of Cashmere's story in distinguishing the company from its competitors. Market research firm Euromonitor International found in its Lifestyles Survey 2017 that "brands that have unique founder stories present a point of differentiation while also emphasizing purpose—factors that tend to resonate more with Millennial consumers than other generations."[290]

Additionally, Beauty Bakerie diverged from the beauty industry's status quo in terms of its messaging about inclusivity. The Fenty Effect pressured many cosmetics companies to prioritize expansive shade ranges in the foundation and concealer categories, and Beauty Bakerie decided to go even further in embracing dark-skinned women. Although the industry standard has long been to order complexion

---

288 Jean Ginzburg, "'Study, Never Stop Looking for More Information' with Cashmere Nicole," Medium, August 16, 2018.

289 *Jackie Aina*, "Full Face of Women-Owned Beauty Brands," November 21, 2017, video, 21:06.

290 Kayla Villena, "Millennial Beauty," Euromonitor International, January 23, 2019.

products in order from lightest to darkest, Beauty Bakerie was the first to label its shades from darkest to lightest.[291]

As Cashmere explained, this move spoke to black women because product order usually favors fairer shades. "But for dark skinned women, how does it feel to have to always reach to the back of the shelf? To have to bend down when we go to Sephora or Ulta, or when we're on a website and we have to keep scrolling to the bottom to find our shade?"[292]

Beauty Bakerie also made sure to prioritize dark skin beyond its thirty-shade foundation and eighteen-shade concealer. Many companies, including those with extensive ranges in liquid products, neglect dark complexions when formulating powers. Although Beauty Bakerie is still growing, it has already released richly pigmented shades for dark complexions in its setting powders, blushes, and highlighters. Its popular "Coffee & Cocoa" palette also features a bronzer shade that runs very deep, which is rare to find in the industry. This was important to Cashmere because her daughter, whose skin is darker than hers, always struggled to find complexion products.[293]

Beauty Bakerie is the model of a company that leverages uniqueness in its packaging, origin story, and approach to

---

[291] Bella Cacciatore, "Cashmere Nicole Is What a 2019 CEO Looks Like," *Glamour*, August 13, 2019.

[292] Ethan D'Spain, "Beauty Bakerie's Cashmere Nicole Is Better, Not Bitter," *Paper*, December 4, 2018.

[293] Shammara Lawrence, "Beauty Bakerie CEO Cashmere Nicole Opens Up About the Inclusive Indie Makeup Brand's Massive Success," *Allure*, May 1, 2018.

inclusivity to stand out from a digital sea of cosmetics on social media. Aided by a seed funding of $3 million in 2017 and a Series A funding of $4.6 million in 2018, the company achieved a valuation of $40 million in August 2019. Two of its investors are Unilever and New Voices Fund, the latter of which helps female entrepreneurs of color. Additional contributors are black executives like Kenneth Chenault, former CEO of American Express; William Lewis, managing director of investment banking at Lazard; and Charles Phillips, former CEO of software company Infor.[294][295][296]

Anna Ohlsson-Baskerville, the director at Unilever Ventures who led the investment in Cashmere's business, revealed that Beauty Bakerie's quirky approach to branding and its "highly-engaged and inclusive Millennial customer base" had aroused the interest of Unilever. She praised Cashmere for "creating an authentic brand with a distinctive playful positioning."[297]

Meanwhile, Kenneth Chenault lauded Cashmere's tenacity, affirming, "Beauty Bakerie's story is one of perseverance and survival, led by a truly passionate and creative CEO."[298]

---

294 Amy Feldman, "How A Single Mom Battling Breast Cancer Built Beauty Bakerie To A $5M Brand, Got Unilever To Invest," *Forbes*, December 3, 2017.

295 "Series A—Beauty Bakerie Cosmetics Brand," Crunchbase, July 9, 2018.

296 Bella Cacciatore, "Cashmere Nicole Is What a 2019 CEO Looks Like," *Glamour*, August 13, 2019.

297 Amy Feldman, "How A Single Mom Battling Breast Cancer Built Beauty Bakerie To A $5M Brand, Got Unilever To Invest," *Forbes*, December 3, 2017.

298 Nicole Pelletiere, "How Beauty Bakerie Founder Cashmere Nicole Went from Food Stamps to Launching a Multi-Million Dollar Cosmetics Brand," *ABC News*, October 8, 2018.

Beauty Bakerie's divergences from the prevailing current of the beauty industry have propelled Cashmere to a level of success that challenges deep-rooted perceptions of entrepreneurship. ProjectDiane2018, a United States biennial demographic study authored by digitalundivided, found that only twelve black women in 2015 and thirty-four black women in 2017 were each able to raise over $1 million in venture capital funding. When excluding the thirty-four women who received more than $1 million in 2017, the average raised by black women that year was only $42,000. In comparison, Crunchbase reported that the average seed round for all startups in that year was $1.14 million.[299]

To attract investors in this profoundly exclusionary atmosphere, Cashmere went against the grain of her industry. She tapped into young peoples' desire to find special and visually exciting products in a crowded marketplace and she established a personal connection with them by sharing her deepest vulnerabilities. Though not yet a member of the billionaire club, Beauty Bakerie is truly a unicorn of the beauty industry. Built by a self-made woman who expertly conveys her creativity and story, the company has convinced young consumers to stop mid-scroll and pay attention.

Whether it is through setting powders encased in flour bags, uplifting messages from Cashmere, or a comprehensive approach to inclusivity, Beauty Bakerie is a courageous trailblazer.

---

299 "ProjectDiane2018," Digitalundivided, accessed May 30, 2020.

PART III

ANTICIPATING THE FUTURE

CHAPTER 13

THE DILEMMA OF INFLUENCER-CEOS

On May 23, 2019, Jaclyn Hill released a YouTube video that her audience of millions had been anticipating for years. Wearing a full face of makeup and a black and white blouse, she bubbled with joy as she announced that she was launching her own company. The video, titled "Introducing Jaclyn Cosmetics," began with Jaclyn declaring, "By the end of this, I want you guys to walk away feeling like you know my brand, you trust my brand, and I've given you all the information that you need." She beamed as she held up a reflective, white box housing twenty nude lipsticks, illuminated by LED lights and framed by loose plastic diamonds.[300]

Twenty days later, Jaclyn was back in front of the camera. This time, she was living a nightmare.

---

300 *Jaclyn Hill*, "Introducing Jaclyn Cosmetics," May 23, 2019, video, 35:39.

Bare-faced and wearing a gray hoodie in this June video, Jaclyn tried to visually signal her vulnerability as she discussed her failed launch. She began by declaring, "The first thing that I want to address before anything else is the accusations that my lipsticks are expired, moldy, or hazardous." She defended herself against these specific allegations before apologizing for the plethora of problems that her lipsticks undeniably had. This video, titled "My Lipsticks," was a far cry from the glitzy and jubilant one that she released in May.[301] With over seven million views, it surpassed her "Introducing Jaclyn Cosmetics" launch video by three million.

All of the top comments, each liked by thousands of people, lambasted her for deceiving her audience with misinformation and deflecting blame with excuses. One of them perfectly summarized the general public opinion toward the video with the words, "She is reaching the word count but not answering the essay question."

Jaclyn's case is an early indicator of the challenges that lie ahead for influencer-CEOs. Though her company is the first of its kind to be so widely castigated for betraying the trust of subscribers, in an industry in which increasingly more influencers are starting their own ventures, it probably will not be the last. The failed Jaclyn Cosmetics launch serves as a warning for influencer-CEOs: while their deeply personal connection with subscribers provides a dedicated customer base, it also requires them to prioritize reciprocal loyalty and integrity to their supporters.

---

301 *Jaclyn Hill*, "My Lipsticks," June 12, 2019, video, 14:02.

This is where Jaclyn went wrong. Originally known as a relatable influencer who had been a part of the beauty scene on YouTube almost since its beginning, she fell from grace by abandoning her community.

Jaclyn began to upload tutorials to YouTube in 2012, and her energetic personality and thorough teaching style drew millions of people to her channel.[302] For years, she solidified her reputation as a dynamic and trustworthy presence on the platform. In a nutshell, she was an older sister to the people who watched her videos.

The devotion of her subscribers bred financial success as Jaclyn began partnering with cosmetic companies to create products. On New Year's Day in 2015, she released a collaboration with Morphe that compiled all of her favorite already-existing eyeshadow singles into one palette. Morphe's website crashed as a result of the increased traffic volume, and after coming back online, the palette promptly sold out. Later that same year, Jaclyn collaborated with Becca to create a new highlighter shade, Champagne Pop. In a matter of twenty minutes, Sephora sold a record-breaking twenty-five thousand compacts of the new hue. The limited edition highlighter was so popular that it became a part of Becca's permanent collection and is the best-selling shade.[303]

---

302 Allison Collins, "Facetime With Jaclyn Hill, Vlogger and Social Media Influencer," *WWD*, June 29, 2016.

303 Petra Guglielmetti, "Everything Jaclyn Hill Touches Sells Out Instantly," *Glamour*, January 5, 2016.

These successful partnerships, each garnering millions of dollars in sales, prompted *Glamour* to write that "everything Jaclyn Hill touches sells out instantly."[304]

However, Morphe soon faced an increasingly negative public sentiment toward its product quality and private labelling past, and many of Jaclyn's subscribers became suspicious of her overwhelming promotion of the company's products. She held her ground, going on to release multiple collaborations with Morphe.

One such partnership was the 2018 Vault collection of four palettes, which was marred by drama over the inconsistent quality of some eyeshadows. As Chapter 7 of this book recounted, the problems with the Vault collection began when Morphe sent out the palettes for free to influencers in public relations (PR) packages before they became available for sale. This customary practice encourages influencers to review the products on their channels and incite early excitement among subscribers. At least, this is the intended purpose. In the case of the Vault, millions of viewers saw influencers struggle with the patchiness of the Morphe eyeshadows in videos posted mere days before the launch.[305]

Morphe pushed back the launch date a few weeks, claiming it was ordering improved batches of the palettes.[306] Though Marlena Stell, the CEO of cosmetic company Makeup Geek,

---

304 Ibid.

305 *Jackie Aina*, "Jaclyn Hill x Morphe Vault: They Almost Had Me In the First Half Not Gonna Lie," June 17, 2018, video, 17:42.

306 Laura Capon, "Morphe Has Delayed the Launch of Their Jaclyn Hill Vault Collection after Poor YouTube Reviews," *Cosmopolitan*, June 22, 2018.

asserted in a now-deleted tweet that it was logistically impossible to create and receive these new products from China in the allotted time, Morphe stood by its claim. To this day, there are still questions about what actually occurred behind the scenes.

What is certain is that Jaclyn's involvement in the Vault foreshadowed the chaos that would occur with her own company.

When it came time for the release of Jaclyn Cosmetics in May 2019, everything seemed to go according to plan as the website launched and most of the lipstick shades sold out in under twenty-four hours.[307] Jaclyn's supporters eagerly waited for their products to arrive, expecting the perfection that she had promised in her announcement video.

Whether intentionally or not, Jaclyn's PR packages did not ship to influencers before the lipsticks became available for sale; instead, they all arrived days after the lipsticks went live on the website.[308] If this was intentional on Jaclyn's part, this is unsurprising given that early PR packages had resulted in the drama over the Vault collection in 2018. She may have chosen to avoid the gamble of giving anybody an early look at her products, instead sending the PR packages at the same time as her customers' purchased packages. As a result, her followers had no frame of reference for how the lipsticks would perform.

---

307 Shea Simmons, "Are Jaclyn Hill's So Rich Lipsticks Sold Out? Here's What's Left From The First Launch," *Bustle*, May 31, 2019.

308 Amanda Krause, "A Complete Timeline of Beauty YouTuber Jaclyn Hill's Disastrous Lipstick Launch," *Insider*, June 14, 2019.

The first sign of trouble materialized when a customer tweeted a complaint about the texture of her lipstick. Jaclyn publicly responded with a snarky comment, insinuating that the bizarre texture was caused by a user error on the woman's part: "You posted swatches two days ago loving the lipsticks? Now you're wondering why it's lumpy? It's obvious this lipstick is used and not fresh from factory. Like any other lipstick, if you use it over other products, have dry lips, etc., things like this can happen."[309]

Subsequently, more complaints appeared. Some people shared photos on Twitter of white fuzz and hairs embedded in their lipsticks. Others showed lipsticks with small black dots, a gritty texture, and unidentified small spheres buried within.[310]

In a YouTube video that has been watched more than four million times, influencer RawBeautyKristi analyzed the defective lipsticks under a microscope. Magnified images of fuzz, hairs, dots, and hard spheres in the lipsticks disgusted viewers and further fueled the emerging public outcry. People in the comments section of the video wondered if the lipsticks were expired and if the white strands of fuzz were a type of fungus growing inside the products.[311]

Kristi also remarked on the differing quality between her PR package and the package that she had purchased herself:

---

309 Ibid.

310 Ibid.

311 *RawBeautyKristi*, "The Truth About Jaclyn Hill Cosmetics Lipstick," June 8, 2019, video, 52:16.

"There's a theory going around out there that the purchased lipsticks are different than PR lipsticks...maybe there is a difference between what they send to influencers and what they send the general public...I don't know if this is the case for this or if maybe just the purchase package ended up being worse, but...I can tell you from looking at them that the purchased ones...are way hairier and more problematic in their formulas."[312]

In response, Jaclyn uploaded the "My Lipsticks" video four days later. She claimed that the white fuzz had shed off of cotton gloves worn by employees in the laboratory, the holes had been created by large air bubbles, and the grittiness and hard spheres had resulted from insufficient melting of ingredients. She did not apologize until the 5:42 minute mark, which was almost halfway through the 14:02 minute video. In the comments, people accused Jaclyn of being defensive, lying, and failing to address the multitudes of concerns in full.[313]

Marlena Stell, long-standing influencer and CEO of Makeup Geek, argued on Twitter that she had never seen a cosmetics laboratory use cotton gloves; nitrile and vinyl gloves, which do not shed, are the industry norm.[314] She also released a now-deleted YouTube video titled "Dear Influencers," divulging that she had warned Jaclyn from the beginning against using the particular laboratory in which the Jaclyn Cosmetics

---

312 Ibid.
313 *Jaclyn Hill*, "My Lipsticks," June 12, 2019, video, 14:02.
314 *Marlena Stell*, Twitter post, June 9, 2019.

lipsticks were manufactured. Apparently, that lab had a reputation of quality control issues.³¹⁵

This video was the straw that broke the back of subscriber loyalty.

Jaclyn was accused of being a sell-out and betraying her fans. Articles referred to the fiasco as "Lipstick-Gate," a reference to the media's use of the suffix "-gate" to denote scandals. A petition was created asking her to recall the lipsticks for contamination and safety concerns, and it amassed almost thirty thousand signatures.³¹⁶

On June 22, Jaclyn announced that every customer who purchased a lipstick would receive a full refund.³¹⁷ Then, she deleted her Instagram and Twitter accounts for nearly a month and went silent on YouTube.³¹⁸ The lack of response incited a sentiment of abandonment among her subscribers. Since the lipsticks still had not been recalled, many customers did not know whether they were safe to continue to use. The company's customer service team responded to the influx

---

315 *Tea Spill*, "Marlena Stell EXPOSES the Beauty Community," June 27, 2019, video, 11:26.
316 "Recall Jaclyn Cosmetics," Change.org, accessed May 31, 2020.
317 Thatiana Diaz, "Jaclyn Hill Is Giving Every Person Who Bought Her Lipstick A Refund," *Refinery29*, June 24, 2019.
318 Lauren Rearick, "Jaclyn Hill Deleted Her Social Media Following the Controversial Release of Her Jaclyn Hill Cosmetics Lipstick Line," *Teen Vogue*, July 3, 2019.

of concerns with delays, and Jaclyn's followers felt that she simply did not care about them.[319]

The trust between influencer and subscriber had shattered.

Eventually, Jaclyn returned to social media in a YouTube video titled "Where I've Been." She had the following message to share with the people who had supported her for years: "I built my entire career on my relationship with you guys, and that relationship is so important to me...I love you guys and I value the friendship that I have built with you. You guys have been through so much with me...my anxiety, my depression, I opened up about my abusive relationship in the past, I talked to you guys about my divorce."[320]

Nonetheless, this appeal to sentimentality fell short for many. The damage was deep: Jaclyn publicly criticized the first customer who spoke out about the lipstick contamination on Twitter, refused to recall the products, posted an apology video in which she did not apologize until almost midway through, and went silent without any further explanations for weeks.

Jaclyn Cosmetics is a critical venture to analyze in order to understand what will shape the future of beauty entrepreneurship. The industry is expanding to include more influencer-CEOs, and Jaclyn Cosmetics reveals a potential pitfall of their business models.

---

[319] Abeni Tinubu, "Why Jaclyn Hill Fans Are Hesitant To Forgive Her For The Lipstick Drama," Showbiz Cheat Sheet, September 24, 2019.

[320] *Jaclyn Hill*, "Where I've Been," July 23, 2019, video, 19:02.

The core customer audience that influencer-CEOs target are their own subscribers, who want to support their ventures because they feel authentically close to these YouTubers. For years, influencers have fostered a relationship with their viewers based on friendship, relatability, and unbiased recommendations. Yet the dynamics of this personal connection can be threatened when an influencer launches her own company. Since her new role positions her as the sole driver of sales for her products, the relationship that she has with her subscribers becomes more overtly transactional than when she had only been recommending other companies' items.

When the weight of her business rests entirely on her shoulders, it is a delicate balance to strike between advocating for her venture and remaining unequivocally faithful to her followers.

Since YouTube has proved to be a highly lucrative platform in the past few years, viewers within and outside of the beauty community now recognize the power of their support. As *The Independent* indicated, "consumers are becoming ever more savvy about the problematic ways some influencers choose to make money…Where once a YouTuber's name was a fool-proof way to sell millions, it's now a sure-fire way to face the kind of scrutiny and criticism few brands could endure."[321]

Subscribers' self-awareness demands true reciprocity between them and influencers. Unfortunately, influencer-CEOs are

---

321 Sirena Bergman, "How Jaclyn Hill's Lipstick Scandal Could Transform the YouTube Make-up Industry Forever," *The Independent*, June 14, 2019.

especially liable to prioritize the venture that bears their name at the cost of their viewers' trust.

Nevertheless, this tendency *can* be resisted.

Example of successful influencer-founded businesses do exist; Krave Beauty, Makeup Geek, and Tati Beauty are all owned by women with long and substantial careers on YouTube. While none of them was forced to contend with a quality control disaster on such a monumental scale, they have each experienced their own hiccups. The fundamental difference between them and Jaclyn Cosmetics is that their founders' blueprint for overcoming public obstacles was based on transparent and constant communication. This principle allowed them to project integrity and fidelity to subscribers, garnering sympathy in the face of setbacks.

Even Jaclyn Cosmetics could have escaped much of the fallout if its founder had followed this model. As some people in the comments of Jaclyn's videos suggested, she should have aligned herself with her fans and shifted the blame onto the laboratory from the beginning. Instead, when the influx of concerns began, Jaclyn chose to position the conflict between herself and her subscribers.

To date, Jaclyn Cosmetics has had only one more launch: a highlighter collection released before Thanksgiving in 2019. It was met with some resistance, but compared to the lipstick collection that the company eventually stopped selling, the release was tame. The main accusation in the comments section of Jaclyn's video revealing the highlighters for the first time was that Jaclyn only returns to YouTube when she has something to sell to her subscribers.[322] This rebuke certainly appears justified given that in the third video after the highlighter reveal, she was announcing another new collaboration palette with Morphe.[323]

Although Jaclyn Cosmetics is still in business, Jaclyn is facing an uphill battle. What could have been an instantly successful company is now one with an uncertain future. Even worse, Jaclyn is seen as traitor to the very people who elevated her to fame and fortune. Before the scandal, her YouTube subscriber count had been gaining between twenty-five thousand and one hundred twenty-five thousand subscribers per month; since Lipstick-Gate, it has been steadily decreasing by about ten thousand people per month.[324] This trend is particularly troubling for Jaclyn Cosmetics because its main marketing platform is its founder's YouTube channel.

Certainly, there are some who want to see Jaclyn redeem herself; after all, the company is still afloat because some people purchased from the highlighter collection. Nonetheless, there is much work to be done before the beauty community can trust Jaclyn again.

Unlike most entrepreneurs, influencer-CEOs do not build faceless companies. With an already-existing customer base of eager fans, they naturally use their following as a springboard for their ventures. They leverage the personal

---

322 *Jaclyn Hill*, "Jaclyn Cosmetics Holiday Collection Reveal," November 14, 2019, video, 32:49.

323 *Jaclyn Hill*, "The Jaclyn Hill Palette Volume 2 Reveal + Swatches," February 10, 2020, video, 33:25.

324 "Jaclyn Hill," Social Blade, accessed May 31, 2020.

connections that they have nurtured for years with viewers who genuinely want to help them achieve their dreams. Yet the risks are great. Social media amplifies consumers' condemnation just as much as it does their approval. It serves as a tool of accountability that unites millions of voices, rapidly changing the tide of public opinion.

As Jaclyn demonstrated, the challenge that lies ahead for the increasing number of influencer-CEOs is to stay true to the people who made them. These followers are the bedrock of YouTubers' success, and the dishonest exploitation of their support is the ultimate betrayal.

The elasticity of subscriber loyalty has been tested, and viewers have responded with enduring distrust of Jaclyn. The road to redemption is long for an influencer who seemingly put their safety on the back burner.

CHAPTER 14

CHALLENGES TO CONSUMERISM

"Does this item spark joy within you?"

This central question frames the KonMari method devised by Marie Kondo, a Japanese organizing consultant and author. If an item does not spark joy, the owner should thank it for being a part of her life and donate it to somebody else. With this philosophy, Marie's objective is to orient people toward mindfulness when they contemplate future purchases, ensuring that they only bring items that they genuinely value into their lives.[325]

Marie introduced the method to the world in 2014 through the book *The Life-Changing Magic of Tidying Up*, which has been purchased by over ten million people worldwide and translated in forty-two languages.[326]

---

325 "About KonMari," KonMari, accessed May 31, 2020.
326 "KonMari Books," Sunmark Publishing, accessed May 31, 2020.

The book challenges excessive consumerism with a simple yet revolutionary message: joy is not ignited by simply possessing an item. Regardless of what that product is, it must offer something beyond mere ownership for it to induce happiness. In short, the KonMari method resists the trend toward mindless acquisition that is encouraged by retail therapy.

Unsurprisingly, this has touched a nerve in the United States; by January 2018, *The Life-Changing Magic of Tidying Up* had been on the *New York Times* best-seller list for 144 weeks.[327] In January 2019, Netflix released a show called *Tidying Up With Marie Kondo*. In each episode, Marie enters an American family's home to help them part with the clutter that has overtaken their lives.[328]

Marie's philosophy of tidying has even permeated the beauty community, resonating with consumers and influencers who are overwhelmed by the industry's increasingly maximalist tendencies. In recent years, makeup companies have adopted fast fashion approaches that prioritize constant releases and short-lived fads. These practices have induced over-saturation in the marketplace, consequently spurring product exhaustion. Instead of eagerly anticipating each launch and envisioning the ways in which it can be used to express creativity, many people are simply tired.

As influencer Laura Lee reminisced in a video titled "Huge Anti Haul | Makeup I Will Not Be Buying," MAC Cosmetics's

---

327 "Advice, How-To & Miscellaneous Books—Best Sellers," *The New York Times*, January 20, 2018.

328 Sarah Archer, "*Tidying Up With Marie Kondo* Isn't Really a Makeover Show," *The Atlantic*, January 4, 2019.

collections were so rare in previous years that she eagerly waited for them in lines that curled around city blocks. In front of more than 400 thousand viewers, Laura declared that she is no longer excited about the company's launches because "in three days they'll have a new collection, and in three more days they'll have another new collection."[329]

This sentiment of product fatigue is reflected in a research note published by UBS, a global financial services firm. UBS analysts explained that "The deceleration in prestige cosmetics sales started when Marie Kondo's book, *The Life-Changing Magic of Tidying Up*, began to soar in popularity…We think that this movement could have had an impact on cosmetics purchasing habits. Consumers may have elected to purchase just the products they need as opposed to hoarding palettes and amassing a wardrobe of lipsticks and mascaras."[330]

Cue the drag queen Kimberly Clark. Inspired by Marie Kondo's ideology, she began to apply the KonMari method to the beauty industry.

Since 2015, Kimberly has released a series of anti-haul videos inspired by beauty influencers' habit of showcasing their "hauls" in front of their viewers. According to Andi Zeisler, co-founder of feminist magazine *Bitch Media*, "understanding anti-hauls requires rewinding to YouTube's early days, when 'haul' videos helped put the video-sharing site on the

---

329 *Laura Lee*, "Huge Anti Haul | Makeup I Will Not Be Buying," October 27, 2019, video, 24:24.

330 Hayley Peterson, "VSCO Girls Are Upending the Cosmetics Industry by Eschewing Makeup in Favor of Facial Sprays and Creams," *Business Insider*, October 23, 2019.

cultural map and establish it as a place for amateur creators to thrive." Typical haul videos consist of YouTubers unpacking their purchases from a shopping spree and filming their commentary on each product.[331]

Kimberly's videos follow the same format of analyzing items, but their objective is to pull back the marketing curtain of consumerism and reveal the negative aspects of products. She specifies launches that she will *not* purchase from because they are mundane, confusing, expensive, or similar to what she already owns. Occasionally, Kimberly discusses specific companies she refuses to support because of their questionable ethics or their founders' negative behaviors.[332]

Her message applies Marie Kondo's framework to beauty: Kimberly argues that makeup lovers must stop shopping in such monumental quantities. Her catchphrase, "I don't need it and I'm not going to buy it," encourages customers to look past the tempting marketing of cosmetics companies and consider the utility of products in their own lives. The phrase rejects the notion that we are defined by what we possess; instead, she declares that products are defined by our use for them.

When Kimberly began her series, influencers were generally hauling the few purchases that they themselves had made; now, many of their homes are flooded by PR packages every week. This is especially true of influencers with large followings,

---

[331] Andi Zeisler, "Are Anti-Hauls the Antidote to YouTube's Cult of Consumerism," *Bitch Media*, June 18, 2019.

[332] *Kimberly Clark*, "Best of Antihauls!—Helpful Tips, Rants and Reads," September 28, 2017, video, 33:11.

who must contend with hundreds of boxes appearing at their doorsteps. The influx of products has become unrelenting as companies scramble to pump out trends as rapidly as they can. This hysteria is exemplified by the waves of limited edition collections that appear for every possible holiday. Many of these are the result of exclusive partnerships with influencers who help to sell out the products.

But enough is enough for many.

Kimberly's anti-haul idea swept through the beauty community in 2017 as influencers with millions of subscribers began to do their own anti-hauls. This was the first major resistance on YouTube to a culture of excessive consumerism.

The popularity of anti-hauls is especially fascinating because influencers' incomes are largely dependent on discount codes, affiliate links, and sponsorships. All of these sources generate more revenue as influencers convince more of their viewers to purchase the products that they recommend. Therefore, one would expect them to rejoice at the inundation of the marketplace and the endless items that they can feature in their videos.

Despite this logic of self-interest, some influencers are taking a public stand against the torrent of launches. They are arguing that product exhaustion is stifling creativity and overwhelming them.

One such example is Samantha Ravndahl, who released a video in November 2018 stating that she would be removing herself from every beauty company's PR list because she no longer wanted to be inundated with free products. This video, named "No More PR," received more than 400 thousand views and spurred other influencers, like Lauren Curtis, to remove themselves from many PR lists as well.[333], [334]

Samantha explained that one of the reasons for her decision was that she hoped that "this makes makeup fun again." She clarified, "When I was younger, I used to buy makeup and absolutely covet it...I would use it in as many ways as possible and I had an inventory of everything that I had in my collection because they all meant something...The novelty has really worn off for me."

Another reason was the environmental impact associated with continually discarding elaborate packaging and endlessly accumulating products that expire before she has time to use them. Samantha remarked, "I probably donate or give away close to 80 percent of what I receive in PR. And then there's the 20 percent that I set aside, some of which I use [only] once, a large portion of which I actually don't ever end up using." She also demonstrated examples of packaging waste: one perfume came packaged in four different boxes stacked inside one another, a few small makeup items arrived in box that was several feet tall, and some PR packages could not be placed in normal recycling bins because they contained mini TV screens that played the campaign commercials for the products within.[335]

---

333 *Samantha Ravndahl*, "No More PR," November 16, 2018, video, 24:17.

334 *Lauren Curtis*, "Goodbye PR Packages … Makeup Cull," November 28, 2018, video, 8:12.

335 *Samantha Ravndahl*, "No More PR," November 16, 2018, video, 24:17.

Since publishing the video, Samantha has maintained her stance on PR, choosing to transition away from having a channel dominated by reviews of all of the newest launches. When she does want to test a product for her subscribers, she simply purchases it herself.

Going a step further, Samantha has also completed a three-month "no-buy."[336] Influencers who partake in this challenge refuse to purchase cosmetic products for a certain time period so that they are forced to use up items that they already have at home. While this may seem like a simple task, it is anything but convenient to a YouTuber whose livelihood depends on experimentation with makeup. Another variant of this is the "project pan" challenge, in which influencers attempt to use up their powder products until they hit the metal pan at the bottom; if they are using products so much that they begin to see the pan, this generally means that they have scaled back their purchases so that they can focus on using up what they already own.

Admittedly, the groups that partake in these instances of pushback against consumerism are a minority of the beauty community. Although Samantha has almost a million followers, the rest of the influencers that challenge themselves to "no-buys" and "project pans" generally have a significantly smaller following. Additionally, these challenges are also limited in scope by necessity—influencers would run out of content to film if they refused to buy new products indefinitely.

---

336 *Samantha Ravndahl*, "Three Month No Buy ... How Did That Go," December 31, 2019, video, 19:25.

Nonetheless, their message is powerful. By demonstrating that they can create beautiful and varied makeup looks with the tools that they already possess, they promote the idea that beauty routines should be artistic rather than overwhelming. In an industry driven by mass consumption, their videos are proof that it is possible to express oneself without stressfully obsessing over incessant acquisition.

Meanwhile, influencer RawBeautyKristi addressed another side of beauty's excessive consumerism: the culture of limited edition products. In a video titled "Makeup I Am Not Going to Buy...Anti-Haul," which has over 800 thousand views, she shared her frustration that many launches "aren't stand-alone holy grail products that are going to make their way into everyone's permanent collection. So many products now are limited edition that they're not being created necessarily to stay in the [cosmetics] line and still be your favorite product five years from now."[337]

Kristi's commentary alludes to two problems with the limited edition model.

Since these products come and go in a blip of time, companies generally do not invest in their quality as they would a product that is meant to satisfy consumers for many years. People who collect limited edition products are probably already avid fans of either the company or the influencer who collaborated on the project. As a result, they are an inherently easier audience to please than the wide assortment of

---

337 *RawBeautyKristi*, "Makeup I Am Not Going to Buy ... Anti-Haul," October 17, 2019, video, 31:59.

customers who purchase from a company's permanent collections throughout the years.

Additionally, this model ignites a purchasing frenzy among consumers who dread that a product will inevitably sell out and never return. They especially feel pressured to buy limited edition items when their favorite influencers are associated with them. Influencers fuel the fire, warning their subscribers that they may miss their opportunity to purchase. In reality, many companies deceive consumers with the tactic of scarcity marketing, which involves intentionally offering low amounts of stock for the first launch so that the product sells out very quickly. The companies then offer the rest of the stock bit by bit in subsequent rounds of launches, claiming each time that the product will be gone once it sells out. Of course, it is never actually gone until the final round.

In the moment, young customers are driven into a panic. Even if they realize that they are being duped, they still do not know when the final round will be when the product sells out and truly does not return. Rather than purchasing with the idea of adding a product that sparks joy to their collection, many are driven to accumulate because of fear.

Andi Zeisler from *Bitch Media* expounds upon this larger issue of emotional manipulation: Kimberly Clark "and many of the YouTube anti-haulers she's inspired dish about, say, the subpar quality of makeup collections rushed to market, but they also offer a more holistic look at the stark facts of capitalism and consumer psychology—the manufacturing of desire, the artificial scarcity of limited edition products, the plague of FOMO [Fear Of Missing Out]."[338]

As the Netflix investigative docuseries *Broken* revealed in November 2019, these practices have dangerous real-world implications.

Its first episode, named "Makeup Mayhem," chronicled the story of Khue Nong, a young woman whose lips were sealed shut by a Kylie Cosmetics lipstick that contained superglue. Her lips remained stuck together until she painfully scrubbed them free with a mixture of butter and 100 percent acetone nail polish remover. Unbeknownst to her, the lipstick was a counterfeit.

Khue had purchased the Kylie Lip Kit for around $20 from eBay after it had repeatedly sold out on Kylie's website. She was seeking that specific item because she had come across multiple posts of influencers wearing it and she wanted to mimic their makeup artistry. In her words, "You want to look that way. You see that look and you think, 'That's what I have to use' to achieve it."

Following Khue's anecdote in the episode, Lexy Lebsack, senior beauty editor at *Refinery29*, explained the relationship between counterfeit cosmetics goods and artificial scarcity. She asserted, "we're living in…a sell-out culture. A lot of [companies] are using this scarcity tactic where they only produce a small amount, even though the demand is maybe

---

338 Andi Zeisler, "Are Anti-Hauls the Antidote to YouTube's Cult of Consumerism," *Bitch Media*, June 18, 2019.

a little bit larger, to try to drum up excitement for the brand in a very crowded marketplace." As a result, some people are driven to extremes when they cannot obtain items that are intensely promoted on social media.[339]

This is the underbelly of excessive consumerism in the beauty industry. As a result of FOMO, some consumers are turning to the hazardous world of counterfeit cosmetics.

Shocked by the docuseries' photographs of horrendously filthy counterfeit labs, influencer Tati Westbrook took matters into her own hands to raise awareness of the issue. In a video called "This Needs To Stop," which has received almost two million views, she revealed pictures of three websites that were selling fake versions of her company's eyeshadow palette. The product had been sold out due to immense demand, and fans were worried that it would never return. In response, Tati emphasized that the palette was *not* limited edition, so everybody who wanted one would eventually have the chance to purchase from Tati Beauty's legitimate website. Tati explained, "I'm not going to even market it that way, where it's like 'buy it now or you'll never get it'…I am going to restock."

She also showed a screenshot of a tweet that she had posted on the day after her company's first launch. It revealed that Tati Beauty had sold out of the initial one hundred thousand eyeshadow palettes that it had manufactured. Tati then explained that she had made as many of the palettes as she

---

[339] "Makeup Mayham," *Broken* Season 1, Episode 1, Netflix, November 27, 2019.

could afford to given that she had to invest her own money for that first launch, and she had offered them all up for sale. She declared, "I am not holding back inventory because I want to create anxiety in the market...That's not what I'm about. I'm about the real fun of makeup."[340]

Accompanied by KonMari-inspired anti-hauls, rejections of free PR packages, and various YouTube challenges rooted in experimenting with products that one already owns, Tati's video is an indicator of the various pockets of resistance that have appeared online. Although these attitudes are certainly not mainstream, many people are visibly pushing back against the direction that the beauty industry has taken.

Eventually, beauty businesses will need to respond. For years, many of them have been laying the groundwork of hyper-consumerism. They have contributed to a perfect storm of perpetual launches fortified by a healthy dose of influencer hype and scarcity marketing. Now that various channels of resistance are emerging, these companies may soon need to temper their extremist marketing tendencies in favor of generating sincere sparks of joy for their launches.

Otherwise, consumers may simply tune out the noise.

---

340 *Tati*, "This Needs to Stop," December 5, 2019, video, 18:00.

CONCLUSION

This is today's culture of beauty.

Fueled by competition, molded by innovation, and nourished by digital content, the beauty industry is a paradigm of business in the twenty-first century.

It has experienced a seismic shift in the past decade as new technologies have united young enthusiasts and engendered beauty's Information Age. The resulting community is remarkably informed and vocal. In the words of Stephan Kanlian, head of a think tank at New York's Fashion Institute of Technology, "I don't think that we've ever seen consumers, certainly in the beauty industry, at such a high level of education and sophistication."[341]

This flourishing community is comprised of Generation Z and Millennial members who recognize their joint power to uplift enterprises that they identify with. A cohort of

---

341 Ahiza Garcia, "The Skincare Industry Is Booming, Fueled by Informed Consumers and Social Media," *CNN*, May 10, 2019.

entrepreneurs has embraced these consumers, effectively challenging the conglomerates that have long dominated the industry. In the current context, beauty is open to anybody who can captivate the hearts, screens, and wallets of young customers.

A trend of democratization has given rise to indie founders, propelled to success by social media and e-commerce. According to Laura Nelson, CEO of Seed Beauty and incubator of Kylie Cosmetics, platforms like Instagram ensure that "information is being directly provided to the consumers so there's less filtering, less editing happening...That really empowers the consumer to make...great purchasing decisions and get different perspectives directly from the brand." Customers are able to immediately act on those decisions through online shopping, whereas "traditionally you had big retailers setting the pace."[342]

This democratized ecosystem of beauty has nurtured special ventures with unique missions. Their visionary founders are navigating a constantly evolving landscape without a definitive blueprint. Through inclusivity, transparency, ethical initiatives, relatability, ingenious content, and imaginative branding, they have discovered means to successfully fill niches in a congested marketplace.

To disseminate their particular ethos, each of these companies cultivates personal connections with young people. They simultaneously leverage their own digital platforms and

---

342 Dayna Winter, "Powering the Pout: The (Other) Woman Behind Kylie Cosmetics," Shopify, May 11, 2017.

those of influencers; this enables them to establish customer-brand reciprocity while also tapping into the deeply loyal audiences of these influencers. This two-pronged approach of communication renders them experts at publicly aligning their brands with desires and values that are important to Generation Z and Millennials.

Carrie Mellage, vice president of consumer products for research firm Kline & Co., refers to indie ventures as "ankle-biters" because they are increasingly taking shares of the industry. In 2019, she explained to *The Wall Street Journal* that "in the past, they were maybe not collectively as much of a threat as they are today."[343]

However, the work of beauty entrepreneurs is far from over. The evolution of beauty exhibits no signs of stopping, guaranteeing a future of persistent creativity governed by the will of Generation Z and Millennials.

One such source of ingenuity is skincare.

According to market research company The NPD Group, "sales of skincare products in the US grew by 13 percent in 2018, hitting $5.6 billion, while makeup sales increased just 1 percent."[344] Inspired by the exportation of Korean skincare regimens, Western customers are becoming more concerned with caring for their base.

---

343 Sara Castellanos, "Estée Lauder Revamps IT, Merging Beauty Business With Innovation," *The Wall Street Journal*, March 20, 2019.

344 Ahiza Garcia, "The Skincare Industry Is Booming, Fueled by Informed Consumers and Social Media," *CNN*, May 10, 2019.

L'Oréal CEO Jean-Paul Agon confirmed this trend in August 2019, commenting, "By category, skincare is leading in every region of the world and in every sector of the market, balancing the slowdown in makeup, particularly in the US and Western Europe."[345] Shifting consumer sentiments explain the monumental success of The Ordinary, Drunk Elephant, and Glossier.

There is much speculation about prospective inventions in the skincare category, including technology that mixes customized formulas to perfectly address an individual's concerns.

Shiseido is exploring the potential of this idea in-store. It launched a machine called Optune in 2018 that scans faces and chooses the best mix of skincare cartridges, effectively 3D printing formulas.[346] If the analysis is accurate, it would remove the process of trial and error that currently defines skincare shopping.

Meanwhile, Procter & Gamble is experimenting with condensing this kind of device to fit into people's bathrooms. Its Olay Moments machine is a small tower that "functions like a skin care Keurig. You insert a pod of a base material, and then based on your personalized skin care needs and

---

345 Hayley Peterson, "VSCO Girls Are Upending the Cosmetics Industry by Eschewing Makeup in Favor of Facial Sprays and Creams," *Business Insider*, October 23, 2019.

346 "How Technology Is Giving the Beauty Industry a Makeover," J.P. Morgan, accessed June 1, 2020.

environmental surroundings, the tower will print custom lotions for your daytime and nighttime routines."[347]

The spirit of innovation is also present in makeup technology. For instance, L'Oréal's subsidiary brand Lancôme has produced a machine that analyzes complexions to find the right color match. Customers' foundations can then be mixed in-store, "with a proprietary algorithm choosing the right shade from thousands of variations."[348] By enabling the products to be immediately manufactured in-store, 3D printing may also reduce the carbon footprint of each customer.[349]

Inevitably, IT teams will become paramount in the race to invent personalized, convenient, and eco-friendly skincare and makeup.

It remains to be seen how indie companies will afford to compete on this front. For now, this technical knowledge and capability is mainly reserved for giants that invest heavily in research and development. Perhaps as this technology becomes more accessible, startups will discover how to integrate it into the brand identity that differentiates each of them from conglomerates.

Even the field of digital marketing, which indie founders have mastered, will pose its own challenges in the future.

---

347 Victoria Song, "Olay Convinced Me to Moisturize By Showing Me What I'll Look Like in 20 Years," Gizmodo, January 9, 2019.

348 "How Technology Is Giving the Beauty Industry a Makeover," J.P. Morgan, accessed June 1, 2020.

349 Sara Castellanos, "Estée Lauder Revamps IT, Merging Beauty Business With Innovation," *The Wall Street Journal*, March 20, 2019.

One bewildering example of what lies ahead is Shudu Gram, a computer-generated model who has baffled Instagram users with her realistic appearance. She appeared on the platform in 2017, introduced through a series of nude photographs in which she bore the neck rings associated with the Ndebele people of South Africa.[350] From then on, she has modeled in publications such as *Harper's Bazaar*, *Vogue*, *Cosmopolitan*, and *WWD*, and she has even promoted Fenty Beauty and Pat McGrath products.[351]

Her architect is the British photographer Cameron-James Wilson, who is white. It takes him several days to develop each post using a 3D modeling program. As he told *Harper's Bazaar*, "She represents a lot of the real models of today. There's a big kind of movement with dark skin models, so she represents them and is inspired by them."[352]

Evidently, Shudu has ignited conversations around the politics of a white man profiting off of the imagery of black women. After all, Wilson's creation, which has more than 200 thousand followers on Instagram, occupies a coveted space in an industry that has long neglected dark-skinned models.

Lauren Michele Jackson, a faculty member at Northwestern University and a PhD recipient in English from the University of Chicago, criticized Shudu in *The New Yorker*. She argued that the android reminds her of a minstrel show,

---

350 Lauren Michele Jackson, "Shudu Gram Is a White Man's Digital Projection of Real-Life Black Womanhood," *The New Yorker*, May 4, 2018.

351 *Shudu.gram*, Instagram, accessed June 1, 2020.

352 Jenna Rosenstein, "People Can't Tell If This Fenty Model Is Real Or Fake," *Harper's Bazaar*, February 9, 2018.

which was a theatrical form in the nineteenth and twentieth centuries in which white musicians known as minstrels painted their faces black and portrayed racist stereotypes of African Americans. As Lauren scrolled through Shudu's Instagram page, she thought of American historian Eric Lott's argument "that blackface minstrels, who originated during the antebellum period, allowed white audiences to indulge their intense fascination with blackness without having to interact with actual black people."[353], [354]

Another example of a digital influencer is Lil Miquela, a Brazilian-American "teenager" whom Pat McGrath has deemed one of her muses.[355] Boasting more than two million followers, she models and produces music for her Generation Z audience. Although she has not faced the degree of resistance that Shudu has, Lil Miquela's popularity raises questions about the future of online marketing and the ethics of creating extremely realistic androids that appeal specifically to impressionable children.

Fenty Beauty and Pat McGrath Labs have already utilized computer-generated models, legitimizing the possibility that other beauty companies will follow suit. However, this foray into android marketing would introduce an interesting paradox into an industry that is increasingly moving toward authenticity and personal connection.

---

353 *Encyclopaedia Britannica*, s.v. "Minstrel Show," May 19, 2020.
354 Lauren Michele Jackson, "Shudu Gram Is a White Man's Digital Projection of Real-Life Black Womanhood," *The New Yorker*, May 4, 2018.
355 Alexa Tietjen, "Influencer Ex Machina," *WWD*, July 11, 2018.

One thing is certain: the metamorphosis of beauty is and will continue to be fascinating.

Beauty has always been deeply tied to identity, serving as a vehicle for self-expression and self-care. As a result, it is viscerally impacted by the changing perspectives of new generations of consumers. Young people are more interconnected than ever before, constantly creating shared culture, uniting through communities, and pushing for change. In a market of seemingly limitless options, they intentionally and selectively support those with unconventional visions and genuine intentions.

In short, they are redefining the role of businesses in modernity.

At the forefront of this thrilling dynamism are indie founders. Their stories of ambition, tenacity, courage, and originality culminate into an extraordinary landscape of entrepreneurship that challenges the status quo.

Together with Generation Z and Millennials, they are crafting a world that is quintessentially twenty-first century.

REFERENCES

INTRODUCTION

Biron, Bethany. "Beauty Has Blown up to Be a $532 Billion Industry—and Analysts Say That These 4 Trends Will Make It Even Bigger." *Business Insider.* July 9, 2019. https://www.businessinsider.com/beauty-multibillion-industry-trends-future-2019-7#1-traditional-retailers-experiment-with-beauty-1.

Gates, Henry Louis. "Madam Walker, the First Black American Woman to Be a Self-Made Millionaire." PBS. Accessed May 28, 2020. https://www.pbs.org/wnet/african-americans-many-rivers-to-cross/history/100-amazing-facts/madam-walker-the-first-black-american-woman-to-be-a-self-made-millionaire/.

Hinchliffe, Emma. "Funding For Female Founders Stalled at 2.2 percent of VC Dollars in 2018." *Fortune.* January 28, 2019. https://fortune.com/2019/01/28/funding-female-founders-2018/.

Thomas, Barbara. "An American Pioneer Is Rediscovered." *Los Angeles Times.* February 15, 1999. https://www.latimes.com/archives/la-xpm-1999-feb-15-cl-8270-story.html.

CHAPTER 1

Bennett, Nomi-Kaie, Amy Rossmeisl, Karisma Turner, Billy Holcombe, Robin Young, Tiffany Brown, and Heather Key. "Parasocial Relationships: The Nature of Celebrity Fascinations." Find a Psychologist. Accessed May 28, 2020. https://www.findapsychologist.org/parasocial-relationships-the-nature-of-celebrity-fascinations/.

Chan, Mi-Anne. "Get Ready: Jaclyn Hill's New Becca Products Are Even Better Than Her Last." *Refinery29*, May 20, 2016. https://www.refinery29.com/en-us/2016/05/111441/jaclyn-hill-becca-cosmetics-champagne-glow-interview.

Clement, J. "YouTube: Annual Beauty Content Views 2018." Statista. December 4, 2019. https://www.statista.com/statistics/294655/youtube-monthly-beauty-content-views/.

Danziger, Pamela. "6 Trends Shaping The Future Of The $532B Beauty Business." *Forbes*. September 1, 2019. https://www.forbes.com/sites/pamdanziger/2019/09/01/6-trends-shaping-the-future-of-the-532b-beauty-business/#4deeeed6588d.

Kang, Jaewon. "Celebrities Like Kylie Jenner Are Upending the $52 Billion Beauty Industry." *The Wall Street Journal*. November 28, 2018. https://www.wsj.com/articles/celebrities-like-kylie-jenner-are-upending-the-52-billion-beauty-industry-1543401001?mod=article_inline.

Social Blade. "Laura Lee." Accessed May 28, 2020. https://socialblade.com/youtube/user/laura88lee.

Mirhaydari, Anthony. "Beauty for All: How Deciem Is Disrupting the Skincare Industry." PitchBook. April 26, 2018. https://pitchbook.com/news/articles/beauty-for-all-how-deciem-is-disrupting-the-skincare-industry.

Terlep, Sharon. "Aging Beauty Brands Want a Facelift." *The Wall Street Journal.* February 5, 2018. https://www.wsj.com/articles/aging-beauty-brands-want-a-facelift-1517826601?mod=article_inline

CHAPTER 2

Aguirre, Abby. "Rihanna Talks Fenty, That Long-Awaited Album, and President Trump." *Vogue.* October 9, 2019. https://www.vogue.com/article/rihanna-cover-november-2019?verso=true.

Alissa Ashley. "Fenty Beauty by Rihanna Review + Tutorial." September 11, 2017. Video, 17:37. https://youtu.be/shzzQxD53Tk.

AP Archive, "Rihanna's Charity Diamond Ball Makes a 'Scary' Move to New York," September 19, 2017, video, 4:59. https://youtu.be/oFCTLrkce8o.

Cruel, Jessica, and Amber Rambharose. "'Nude' Is No Longer One Shade Fits All." *Glamour.* March 21, 2018. https://www.glamour.com/story/nude-makeup-inclusive.

Diaz, Thatiana. "Tarte Is Pulling Its Shape Tape Foundation & Starting Over After Backlash." February 4, 2019. https://www.refinery29.com/en-us/2019/02/223536/tarte-new-face-tape-foundation-shades.

E! Red Carpet & Award Shows. "Rihanna Talks New Fenty Beauty Line at NYFW." September 8, 2017. Video, 2:06. https://youtu.be/iHmur-7Z4cY.

Fenty Beauty by Rihanna. "Artistry & Beauty Talk With Rihanna." July 7, 2019. Video, 29:13. https://youtu.be/K-J_8SCecCg.

Fenty Stats. "Fenty Stats: Awards: Beauty." Accessed May 28, 2020. https://www.fentystats.com/beauty-awards.

Jackie Aina. "Black Girls React to Tarte Shape Tape Foundation." January 16, 2018. Video, 25:28. https://youtu.be/4cXsgT3ZcL8.

Jackie Aina. "Fenty Beauty?! Hot Or Hmmm." September 14, 2017. Video, 23:46. https://youtu.be/2zISrf-7V3U.

Nyma Tang. "Fenty Beauty Pro Filt'r Foundation Review | #thedarkestshade." September 11, 2017. Video, 10:15. https://youtu.be/hQbeBoYXLhs.

Rao, Priya. "The Fenty Effect: How Beauty Brands Are Responding to the New 40-Shade Foundation Standard." Glossy. July 17, 2018. https://www.glossy.co/new-face-of-beauty/the-fenty-effect-how-beauty-brands-are-responding-to-the-new-40-shade-foundation-standard.

Robehmed, Natalie. "How Rihanna Created A $600 Million Fortune—And Became The World's Richest Female Musician." *Forbes.* June 4, 2019. https://www.forbes.com/sites/natalierobehmed/2019/06/04/rihanna-worth-fenty-beauty/amp/.

Rodulfo, Kristina. "For New Foundation Ranges, 'Fenty 40' Is the Magic Number." *Elle.* May 31, 2018. https://www.elle.com/beauty/makeup-skin-care/a20967710/makeup-companies-40-foundation-shades-fenty-beauty-influence/.

Schallon, Lindsay, Rachel Nussbaum, and Teryn Payne. "One Year Later, This Is the Real Effect Fenty Has Had on the Beauty Industry." *Glamour.* September 14, 2018. https://www.glamour.com/story/fenty-beauty-rihanna-legacy.

Snobette. "Rihanna Debuts Fenty Beauty Campaign Ft. Halima Aden, Slick Woods and Leomie Anderson." September 1, 2017. Video, 1:14. https://youtu.be/0_FoFRnZPh4.

Tietjen, Alexa. "Beautyblender's Concealer Launch Strategy? Keep Your Harshest Critics Close." *WWD.* February 5, 2020. https://

wwd.com/beauty-industry-news/beauty-features/beautyblender-influencers-concealer-launch-1203460235/.

Vogue. "Rihanna's Epic 10-Minute Guide to Going Out Makeup | Beauty Secrets." May 3, 2018. Video, 10:28. https://youtu.be/KONe4SNFA64.

CHAPTER 3

Beauty Packaging. "The Ordinary Launches At Ulta Beauty." May 28, 2019. https://www.beautypackaging.com/contents/view_breaking-news/2019-05-28/the-ordinary-launches-at-ulta-beauty/.

Brean, Joseph. "The Inside Story of How Deciem, the Abnormal Beauty Company, Lived up to Its Name." *Financial Post.* November 30, 2018. https://business.financialpost.com/news/retail-marketing/the-inside-story-of-how-deciem-the-abnormal-beauty-company-lived-up-to-its-name.

Bromwich, Jonah Engel. "He Built, Then Nearly Broke, a Successful Beauty Start-Up. Can It Go on Without Him." *The New York Times.* April 17, 2019. https://www.nytimes.com/2019/04/17/style/deciem-brandon-truaxe-ordinary.html.

Cosmetics Business. "How to Launch a Fast-Growing Cosmetics Company." June 17, 2016. https://www.cosmeticsbusiness.com/news/article_page/How_to_launch_a_fastgrowing_cosmetics_company/119001.

Craik, Laura. "Brandon Truaxe: the Man Who Will Change the Way You Buy Beauty." *Evening Standard.* May 4, 2017. https://www.standard.co.uk/lifestyle/esmagazine/brandon-truaxe-the-man-who-will-change-the-way-you-buy-beauty-a3529571.html.

Dr Davin Lim. "Skin Care | Dermatologist Review on The Ordinary." October 14, 2018. Video, 13:06. https://youtu.be/4fjMNGefiXE.

Im, Kelly. "How to 10-Step Your Skincare Regimen like a Korean." *Vogue.* January 10, 2018. https://www.vogue.com.au/beauty/skin/how-to-10step-your-skincare-regimen-like-a-korean/image-gallery/ce47d7b579170c06a4ac39d33b04cfb0.

Mackenzie, Macaela. "Kim Kardashian West Reveals Her Skin-Care Routine, Including The Ordinary's Retinoid Serum." *Allure.* January 26, 2018. https://www.allure.com/story/kim-kardashian-the-ordinary-serum-skin-care-routine.

Mirhaydari, Anthony. "Beauty for All: How Deciem Is Disrupting the Skincare Industry." PitchBook. April 26, 2018. https://pitchbook.com/news/articles/beauty-for-all-how-deciem-is-disrupting-the-skincare-industry.

Molvar, Kari. "Brandon Truaxe of Deciem." *Nuvo.* May 30, 2017. https://nuvomagazine.com/magazine/summer-2017/brandon-truaxe-founder-deciem.

Morosini, Daniela. "Everything You Need To Know About The World's Most Disruptive Beauty Brand." *Refinery29.* July 30, 2017. https://www.refinery29.com/en-gb/2017/07/164157/deciem-founder-brandon-truaxe-interview.

Mpinja, Baze. "Meet Deciem, the Industry-Changing Company Behind The Ordinary Skincare." *Allure.* December 28, 2017. https://www.allure.com/story/everything-you-wanted-to-know-about-deciem.

Nadine Baggott. "Busting Beauty BS With Deciem's Brandon Truaxe." January 7, 2018. Video, 30:32. https://youtu.be/gHuQyVeL3QE.

Pina, Tanisha. "The Skin-Care Industry Is Thriving—but How Long Can This Boom Last." Fashionista. January 24, 2019. https://fashionista.com/2019/01/skin-care-beauty-industry-growth.

Raphael, Rina. "Retailers Big And Small Want A Piece Of The Thriving Korean Beauty Business." *Fast Company*. September 23, 2016. https://www.fastcompany.com/3062673/retailers-big-and-small-want-a-piece-of-the-thriving-korean-beauty-business.

Syme, Rachel. "The Cult Skin-Care Brand Whose Secret Ingredient Is Being Dirt Cheap." *The New Yorker*. January 30, 2018. https://www.newyorker.com/culture/on-and-off-the-avenue/the-ordinary-cult-skin-care-secret-ingredient-is-being-dirt-cheap.

Trefis Team. "Why Estee Lauder Invested In Multi-Brand Skincare Brand Deciem." *Forbes*. June 16, 2017. https://www.forbes.com/sites/greatspeculations/2017/06/16/why-estee-lauder-invested-in-multi-brand-skincare-brand-deciem/#4a5d1e077a27.

CHAPTER 4

Ahlquist, Milly. "A Herbal Heritage: The Story of Lush and Henna Hair Dye." Lush. Accessed May 28, 2020. https://uk.lush.com/article/herbal-heritage-story-lush-and-henna-hair-dye.

Barton, Christine, Lara Koslow, and Christine Beauchamp. "How Millennials Are Changing the Face of Marketing Forever." BCG. January 15, 2014. https://www.bcg.com/publications/2014/marketing-center-consumer-customer-insight-how-millennials-changing-marketing-forever.aspx.

Belam, Martin. "Cosmetics Retailer Lush Criticised by Police over 'Spycops' Ad Campaign." *The Guardian*. June 1, 2018. https://www.theguardian.com/media/2018/jun/01/cosmetics-retailer-lush-criticised-by-police-over-spycops-ad-campaign.

Campaign Opposing Police Surveillance. "An Alliance of People Spied on by Britain's Political Secret Police." February 26, 2020. http://campaignopposingpolicesurveillance.com/.

Chambers, Sam. "Interview: Lush Cosmetics Boss Mark Constantine." *The Times.* May 19, 2019. https://www.thetimes.co.uk/article/interview-lush-cosmetics-boss-mark-constantine-w2rxv0232.

Craft. "Lush Profile." Accessed May 28, 2020. https://craft.co/lush.

Employee Ownership Association. "Lush Announces 10 percent Move to Employee Ownership at EOA Conference." November 27, 2017. https://employeeownership.co.uk/news/8082/.

Giammona, Craig, Carolina Wilson, and Sarah Ponczek. "Investors' Guide to Gen Z: Weed, Social Justice and Kylie Jenner." *Bloomberg.* April 5, 2019. https://www.bloomberg.com/news/articles/2019-04-05/what-s-gen-z-and-how-can-you-invest-cannabis-influencers-key.

Hall, Chloe. "Everything You Need to Know About Lush's Crazy Controversial #Spycops Campaign." *Elle.* June 6, 2018. https://www.elle.com/beauty/a21098901/spycop-lush-cosmetics-explainer/.

Hardy, Jack. "Extinction Rebellion: Climate Protesters Dodge Arrest after Police Run out of Cells." *The Telegraph.* April 16, 2019. https://www.telegraph.co.uk/news/2019/04/16/extinction-rebellion-climate-protesters-dodge-arrest-police/.

Lewis, Paul, Rob Evans, and Rowenna Davis. "Ex-Wife of Police Spy Tells How She Fell in Love and Had Children with Him." *The Guardian.* January 19, 2011. https://www.theguardian.com/environment/2011/jan/19/wife-fourth-police-spy-children.

Lush. "10 Things You Should Know about Lush Packaging." Accessed May 29, 2020. https://www.lushusa.com/stories/article_10-things-lush-packaging.html.

Lush. "Animal Testing: Our Policy." Accessed May 29, 2020. https://uk.lush.com/article/animal-testing-our-policy.

Lush. "Business Should Evolve with Ethics—Mo Constantine." December 23, 2016. Video, 31:30. https://youtu.be/E3Qv8U-8WhNY.

Lush. "Lush Buying Presents: Cocoa Butter." August 28, 2012. Video, 11:48. https://youtu.be/DYt1GuvdQCY.

Lush. "Our Ethical Buying Policy." Accessed May 28, 2020. https://www.lushusa.com/stories/article_our-ethical-buying-policy.html.

Lush. "Source To Skin | Charity Pot." March 29, 2019. Video, 7:15. https://youtu.be/iPq48ubE4HM.

Lush. "The Lush Prize." Accessed May 28, 2020. https://lushprize.org/.

Nielsen. "Was 2018 the Year of the Influential Sustainable Consumer." December 17, 2018.

https://www.nielsen.com/us/en/insights/article/2018/was-2018-the-year-of-the-influential-sustainable-consumer/.

Samadder, Rhik. "Observer Ethical Awards 2014 Winners: Lush." *The Guardian.* June 11, 2014. https://www.theguardian.com/environment/2014/jun/12/observer-ethical-awards-2014-winners-lush.

Saner, Emine. "How the Lush Founders Went from Bath Bombs to the Spy Cops Row." *The Guardian*. June 20, 2018. https://www.theguardian.com/media/2018/jun/20/lush-founders-from-bath-bombs-to-spy-cops-row.

Taylor, Matthew, and Damien Gayle. "Battle of Waterloo Bridge: A Week of Extinction Rebellion Protests." *The Guardian*. April 20, 2019. https://www.theguardian.com/environment/2019/apr/20/battle-of-waterloo-bridge-a-week-of-extinction-rebellion-protests.

TheRichest. "Mark and Mo Constantine Net Worth." Accessed May 28, 2020. https://www.therichest.com/celebnetworth/celebrity-business/celebrity-fashion/mark-and-mo-constantine-net-worth/.

Walters, Kate. "Mark Constantine: Lush." Startups. Accessed May 28, 2020. https://startups.co.uk/mark-constantine-lush/.

Westwater, Hannah. "Lush Founder Mark Constantine Shares His Own Experience of Homelessness." *The Big Issue*. December 20, 2018. https://www.bigissue.com/interviews/lush-founder-mark-constantine-shares-his-own-experience-of-homelessness/.

CHAPTER 5

Amandabb. "Let's Talk About Celebrity Beauty Brands." February 6, 2020. Video, 34:15. https://youtu.be/Co9bIwa-rVc.

Arps, Brianna. "I Used to Get Bullied for Having Naturally Full Lips—but Now That I Love Them, People Accuse Me of Copying Kylie Jenner." *Insider*. July 21, 2017. https://www.insider.com/natural-lips-kylie-jenner-essay-2017-7.

Berg, Madeline. "Billionaire Kylie Jenner To Cash In On Her Cosmetics Line With $600 Million Sale To Coty." *Forbes*.

November 18, 2019. https://www.forbes.com/sites/maddieberg/2019/11/18/billionaire-kylie-jenner-to-cash-in-on-her-cosmetics-line-with-600-million-sale-to-coty/#3b8d87406362.

Chozick, Amy. "Keeping Up With the Kardashian Cash Flow." *The New York Times*. March 30, 2019. https://www.nytimes.com/2019/03/30/style/kardashians-interview.html.

Forbes. "Kylie Jenner." Accessed May 29, 2020. https://www.forbes.com/profile/kylie-jenner/#35d0093955b5.

Kylie Cosmetics. "About." Accessed May 29, 2020. https://www.kyliecosmetics.com/pages/about.

Loose Threads. "Kylie Cosmetics and the Value Paradox of Celebrity Brands." Accessed May 29, 2020. https://loosethreads.com/research/2018/07/17/kylie-cosmetics-and-the-value-paradox-of-celebrity-driven-brands/.

Lovece, Frank. "Kylie Jenner: Plastic Surgery Rumors 'Insulting.'" *Newsday*. April 10, 2014. https://www.newsday.com/entertainment/celebrities/kylie-jenner-plastic-surgery-rumors-insulting-1.7671983.

Mulshine, Molly. "Teenagers on Instagram Are Destroying Their Lips with Shot Glasses in an Attempt to Look like Kylie Jenner." *Business Insider*. April 21, 2015. https://www.businessinsider.com/kylie-jenners-lip-challenge-on-instagram-2015-4.

Robehmed, Natalie. "At 21, Kylie Jenner Becomes The Youngest Self-Made Billionaire Ever." *Forbes*. March 5, 2019. https://www.forbes.com/sites/natalierobehmed/2019/03/05/at-21-kylie-jenner-becomes-the-youngest-self-made-billionaire-ever/#4c981bf82794.

Robehmed, Natalie. "How 20-Year-Old Kylie Jenner Built A $900 Million Fortune In Less Than 3 Years." *Forbes*. July 11, 2018.

https://www.forbes.com/sites/forbesdigitalcovers/2018/07/11/how-20-year-old-kylie-jenner-built-a-900-million-fortune-in-less-than-3-years/#106bbcfcaa62.

Shopify. "The Kylie Cosmetics Story." Accessed May 29, 2020. https://www.shopify.com/kylie?utm_source=post&medium=blog&term=212483913&campaign=kylie.

Schaefer, Kayleen. "Kylie Jenner Built a Business Empire out of Lip Kits and Fan Worship." *Vanity Fair*. October 21, 2016. https://www.vanityfair.com/style/2016/10/kylie-jenner-lip-kits-seed-beauty-colourpop.

Strugatz, Rachel. "Kylie Jenner's Kylie Cosmetics On Way to Becoming $1B Brand." *WWD*. August 9, 2017. https://wwd.com/beauty-industry-news/beauty-features/kylie-jenner-cosmetics-to-become-billion-dollar-brand-10959016/.

CHAPTER 6

Adebowale, Temi. "Pat McGrath's Makeup Line Is Now Worth $1 Billion." *Harper's Bazaar*. July 20, 2018. https://www.harpersbazaar.com/beauty/makeup/a22499334/pat-mcgrath-labs-worth-one-billion/.

Hughes, Sali. "Beauty Queen: How Pat McGrath Became the World's Most Influential Makeup Artist." *The Guardian*. August 6, 2017. https://www.theguardian.com/fashion/2017/aug/06/beauty-queen-how-pat-mcgrath-revolutionised-makeup.

Jackie Aina. "Pat McGrath Has Done It Again?! MotherShip VI Demo." September 18, 2019. Video, 16:02. https://youtu.be/49QEfUXrsEA.

Lang, Cady. "How Renowned Makeup Artist Pat McGrath Is Changing the Face of Beauty On Her Terms." *Time*. September 18, 2017. https://time.com/4945033/pat-mcgrath-unlimited-interview/.

NikkieTutorials. "World's Best Lipsticks." July 12, 2017. Video, 16:45. https://youtu.be/qHR22bRG1-U.

Niven-Phillips, Lisa. "Pat McGrath Labs Becomes Selfridges Biggest-Selling Beauty Line." *The Guardian*. June 1, 2019. https://www.theguardian.com/fashion/2019/jun/01/pat-mcgrath-labs-becomes-selfridges-biggest-selling-beauty-line.

Pat McGrath Labs. "About Pat McGrath Labs." Accessed May 29, 2020. https://www.patmcgrath.com/pages/about-pat-mcgrath-labs.

Pat McGrath Labs. "Pat McGrath Biography." Accessed May 29, 2020. https://www.patmcgrath.com/pages/pat-mcgrath-biography.

Peter, Shannon. "'The Mother of Make-up,' Pat Mcgrath, Reflects on Her Iconic Career." *i-D*. April 11, 2019. https://i-d.vice.com/en_us/article/43jg4q/interview-with-pat-mcgrath-makeup-artist.

Sowray, Bibby. "Pat McGrath." *Vogue*. January 27, 2012. https://www.vogue.co.uk/article/pat-mcgrath-biography.

Tati. "$1,000 Pat McGrath Face." August 9, 2019. Video, 24:45. https://youtu.be/eiXXEly3D08.

Tietjen, Alexa. "Influencer Ex Machina." *WWD*. July 11, 2018. https://wwd.com/beauty-industry-news/beauty-features/influencer-ex-machina-shudu-lil-miquela-virtual-celebrities-instagram-1202755789/.

Wells, Linda. "Pat McGrath Is the Most In-Demand Makeup Artist in the World." *The Cut*. August 8, 2016. https://www.thecut.com/2016/08/pat-mcgrath-makeup-artist-c-v-r.html.

Wolff, Kate. "Beyond Nostalgia: How Brands Can Leverage the Powers of 'Fauxstalgia' and 'Newstalgia.'" *Entrepreneur.* January 14, 2019. https://www.entrepreneur.com/article/326174.

CHAPTER 7

Amandabb. "How Morphe Brushes Changed the Beauty Industry ... (The Problem With Morphe)." March 6, 2020. Video, 36:27. https://youtu.be/_g-fukOLebc.

Brumpton, Harry. "General Atlantic Nears Acquisition of Beauty Brand Morphe." *Reuters.* July 18, 2019. https://www.reuters.com/article/us-morphe-m-a-generalatlantic/general-atlantic-nears-acquisition-of-beauty-brand-morphe-sources-idUSKCN1UD1G2.

Capon, Laura. "Morphe Has Delayed the Launch of Their Jaclyn Hill Vault Collection after Poor YouTube Reviews." *Cosmopolitan.* June 22, 2018. https://www.cosmopolitan.com/uk/beauty-hair/makeup/a21760856/morphe-jaclyn-hill-vault-eyeshadow-palette-bad-reviews-delay-recall/.

General Atlantic. "Morphe Holdings and General Atlantic Announce Partnership and Strategic Growth Investment." August 19, 2019. https://www.generalatlantic.com/media-article/morphe-holdings-and-general-atlantic-announce-partnership-and-strategic-growth-investment/.

Jackie Aina. "Jaclyn Hill x Morphe Vault: They Almost Had Me In the First Half Not Gonna Lie." June 17, 2018. Video, 17:42. https://youtu.be/uVGM7Qz_nOw.

Jaclyn Hill. "August Beauty Favorites." September 4, 2014. Video, 18:12. https://youtu.be/ZAdfx7AZ1NE.

Jaclyn Hill. "Update | Real Talk | A Little About Me | Haters | Makeup Talk." August 19, 2014. Video, 18:40. https://youtu.be/w6INrB38HcA.

James Charles. "James Charles x Morphe Reveal." November 2, 2018. Video, 36:28. https://youtu.be/oc4wxwLbtxo.

Lookfantastic. "#BalanceForBetter: An Interview with the Co-Founders of Morphe." Accessed May 30, 2020. https://www.lookfantastic.com/blog/discover/morphe-exclusive-interview/.

Mansson, Elisabeth. "Sister Stocked? Not A Chance. The James Charles x Morphe Palette Has Sold Out For A Second Time." TheTalko. December 13, 2018. https://www.thetalko.com/the-james-charles-x-morphe-sister-collection-sold-out-second-time/.

Micaela. "Banking on the Influencer Empire: Meet Morphe Cosmetics." Medium. March 11, 2019. https://medium.com/@micaelaf/banking-on-the-influencer-empire-meet-morphe-cosmetics-93815a6f0367.

Morphe. "About Morphe." Accessed May 30, 2020. https://www.morphe.com/pages/about-morphe.

Smokey Glow. "The Truth About Affiliate Links." April 28, 2020. Video, 22:31. https://youtu.be/PQ1skzPcMhI.

Stephanie Nicole. "Morphe Brand Review." February 23, 2016. Video, 25:08. https://youtu.be/PAP6GdyI1B8.

Tati. "Morphe Makeup & Brushes | Hot or Not." December 17, 2015. Video, 13:20. https://youtu.be/ZQCryIKsrAQ.

CHAPTER 8

Amoruso, Sophia, and Huda Kattan. "How to Build a Billion-Dollar Company in 5 Years, According to a Beauty Founder." *Busi-*

ness Insider. October 2, 2019. https://www.businessinsider.com/how-build-billion-dollar-company-5-years-with-huda-kattan-2019-10.

Capon, Laura. "This Is the Beauty Influencer Who Topped This Year's Instagram Rich List." *Cosmopolitan.* July 24, 2018. https://www.cosmopolitan.com/uk/beauty-hair/celebrity-hair-makeup/a22525717/huda-beauty-instagram-rich-list-2018/.

Forbes. "Huda Kattan." September 3, 2019. https://www.forbes.com/profile/huda-kattan/#130eb56d3cec.

Harb, Malak. "For Huda Kattan, Beauty Has Become a Billion-Dollar Business." *The Associated Press.* October 13, 2019. https://apnews.com/c6dd91b4fb8c4d27a151a3a1a5bb8315.

Hopper HQ. "Instagram Rich List 2017—The Platform's Highest-Earners Revealed." November 10, 2017. https://www.hopperhq.com/blog/instagram-rich-list-2017-platforms-highest-earners-revealed/.

Hopper HQ. "Instagram Rich List 2019—Beauty Influencers." Accessed May 30, 2020. https://www.hopperhq.com/blog/instagram-rich-list/niche/beauty/.

Huda Beauty. "How to Shave Your Face (And Why It's Awesome)." April 11, 2016. Video, 4:39. https://youtu.be/md-2UEa99PY.

Huda Beauty. "My Makeup Business Story." October 6, 2016. Video, 14:14. https://youtu.be/Vk41RBKVeh0.

Huda Beauty. "My Story through Feminism! We Should All be Feminist." December 5, 2018. Video, 14:43. https://youtu.be/q0pVevTOnNk.

Imtiaz, Saba. "All Made up! The Indie Makeup Brands That Are Catering to Women of Colour." *The Guardian.* October 30,

2017. https://www.theguardian.com/lifeandstyle/2017/oct/30/indie-makeup-brands-women-of-colour-rihanna-fenty-beauty-huda-kattan-howegrown-cosmetic-major-brands.

Kattan, Huda. "Meet the CEO Who Turned a Makeup Hobby into a Multimillion Dollar Business." Chase. July 25, 2018. https://www.chase.com/news/072418-dream-builders-huda-kattan.

LinkedIn. "Huda Kattan." Accessed May 30, 2020. https://www.linkedin.com/in/hkattan/?originalSubdomain=ae.

McClear, Sheila. "Why Huda Kattan Is One of Beauty's Most Influential Women." *Allure*. June 28, 2017. https://www.allure.com/story/huda-kattan-profile.

NikkieTutorials. "Holy Grail Foundation? Huda Beauty Faux Filter Foundation Review." November 9, 2017. Video, 15:56. https://youtu.be/PuLXfEQsVlM.

Pupic, Tamara. "How Huda, Mona, And Alya Kattan Built Huda Beauty Out Of Dubai." *Entrepreneur*. August 18, 2019. https://www.entrepreneur.com/article/338195.

Shapiro, Bee. "Is Huda Kattan the Most Influential Beauty Blogger in the World." *The New York Times*. March 20, 2017. https://www.nytimes.com/2017/03/20/fashion/is-huda-kattan-the-kim-kardashian-west-of-beauty-bloggers.html.

Sorvino, Chloe. "How Huda Kattan Built A Billion-Dollar Cosmetics Brand With 26 Million Followers." *Forbes*. July 11, 2018. https://www.forbes.com/sites/chloesorvino/2018/07/11/huda-kattan-huda-beauty-billion-influencer/#51758bae6120.

The Business of Fashion. "Huda Kattan | The Power of Being Yourself." December 4, 2018. Video, 9:54. https://youtu.be/VAzbyToc6Yc.

Zahn, Max. "How Beauty Influencer Huda Kattan Learned to Create Viral Posts." Yahoo! Finance. November 7, 2019. https://www.yahoo.com/lifestyle/huda-kattan-instagram-viral-posts-115920261.html.

CHAPTER 9

Bloomberg. "Shiseido to Acquire Drunk Elephant." October 7, 2019. https://www.bloomberg.com/press-releases/2019-10-08/shiseido-to-acquire-drunk-elephant.

Cook, Jeffrey. "Kourtney Kardashian Arrives on Capitol Hill to Clean up Cosmetics." *ABC News.* April 24, 2018. https://abcnews.go.com/Politics/News/kourtney-kardashian-arrives-capitol-hill-clean-cosmetics/story?id=54691855.

Davis, Nicola. "Is Clean Beauty a Skincare Revolution—or a Pointless Indulgence." *The Guardian.* February 4, 2019. https://www.theguardian.com/fashion/2019/feb/04/is-clean-beauty-a-skincare-revolution-or-a-pointless-indulgence.

Drunk Elephant. "Our Philosophy: The Drunk Elephant Difference." Accessed May 30, 2020. https://www.drunkelephant.com/pages/philosophy.

Eldor, Karin. "Drunk Elephant's Founder Shares Expansion Details And Why The Wildly Popular Skincare Brand Is Not Simply 'Clean.'" *Forbes.* September 3, 2019. https://www.forbes.com/sites/karineldor/2019/09/03/drunk-elephants-founder-shares-expansion-details-and-why-the-skincare-brand-is-not-simply-clean/#330123e35157.

Fu, Joanna. "Drunk Elephant Founder Tiffany Masterson on Her 'Suspicious 6' Skincare Philosophy." *Vogue.* November 26, 2019. https://www.voguehk.com/en/article/beauty/drunk-elephant-tiffany-masterson-interview-clean-beauty-skincare/?device=desktop.

Harvard Health Publishing: Harvard Medical School. "By the Way, Doctor: Are Parabens Dangerous." March 2014. https://www.health.harvard.edu/newsletter_article/By_the_way_doctor_Are_parabens_dangerous.

Maloney, Nora. "Drunk Elephant Founder Tiffany Masterson Takes Skincare by Storm." *Vanity Fair*. January 10, 2018. https://www.vanityfair.com/style/2018/01/drunk-elephant-founder-tiffany-masterson-takes-skincare-by-storm.

Masterson, Tiffany. "Founder Note." Drunk Elephant. Accessed May 30, 2020. https://www.drunkelephant.com/pages/about-us.

Milman, Oliver. "US Cosmetics Are Full of Chemicals Banned by Europe—Why." *The Guardian*. May 22, 2019. https://www.theguardian.com/us-news/2019/may/22/chemicals-in-cosmetics-us-restricted-eu.

Rabia. "Beauty Education: The Difference Between Clean, Green, and Natural Beauty Products." Amaliah. March 15, 2019. https://www.amaliah.com/post/47757/trying-to-practice-clean-beauty-here-are-the-6-ingredients-to-avoid.

Sorvino, Chloe. "Hot Skin-Care Brand Drunk Elephant Sells For $845 Million, Minting Founder A Fortune." *Forbes*. October 8, 2019. https://www.forbes.com/sites/chloesorvino/2019/10/08/hot-skincare-brand-drunk-elephant-sells-for-845-million-minting-founder-a-fortune/#2d87586b5140.

Strugatz, Rachel. "Why Shiseido Bought Drunk Elephant." *The Business of Fashion*. October 8, 2019. https://www.businessoffashion.com/articles/beauty/why-shiseido-bought-drunk-elephant.

The NPD Group. "Empowered Consumers Want Clean Ingredients and Brand Transparency from Skincare Products." August 14, 2019. https://www.npd.com/wps/portal/npd/us/news/press-releases/2019/empowered-consumers-want-clean-ingredients-and-brand-transparency-from-skincare-products/.

US Food and Drug Administration. "FDA Advises Consumers to Stop Using Certain Cosmetic Products." October 18, 2019. https://www.fda.gov/cosmetics/cosmetics-recalls-alerts/fda-advises-consumers-stop-using-certain-cosmetic-products.

US Food and Drug Administration. "Statement from FDA Commissioner Scott Gottlieb, M.D., and Susan Mayne, Ph.D., Director of the Center for Food Safety and Applied Nutrition, on Tests Confirming a 2017 Finding of Asbestos Contamination in Certain Cosmetic Products and New Steps That FDA Is Pursuing to Improve Cosmetics Safety." March 5, 2019. https://www.fda.gov/news-events/press-announcements/statement-fda-commissioner-scott-gottlieb-md-and-susan-mayne-phd-director-center-food-safety-and.

Volz, Emily. "Consumer Advocate: Claire's Pulls Children's Makeup after Family Finds Asbestos." *WJAR*. December 22, 2017. https://turnto10.com/i-team/consumer-advocate/claires-pulls-childrens-makeup-after-barrington-family-finds-asbestos.

Wanner, Molly, and Neera Nathan. "Clean Cosmetics: The Science behind the Trend." Harvard Health Publishing: Harvard Medical School. March 4, 2019. https://www.health.harvard.edu/blog/clean-cosmetics-the-science-behind-the-trend-2019030416066.

CHAPTER 10

Berger, Sarah. "Glossier: How This 33-Year-Old Turned Her Beauty Blog to a $1 Billion Brand." *CNBC*. March 30, 2019. https://

www.cnbc.com/2019/03/20/how-emily-weiss-took-glossier-from-beauty-blog-to-1-billion-brand.html.

Branch, Kate. "Emily Weiss on What a Glossier Girl Smells Like and Building a Cool Girl Empire." *Vogue*. September 15, 2017. https://www.vogue.com/article/glossier-emily-weiss-global-london-paris-new-york-body-hero-glossier-you.

Ellison, Jo. "Glossier's Emily Weiss: 'We're Creating the Estée Lauder of the Future.'" *Financial Times*. August 6, 2019. https://www.ft.com/content/352ded56-b509-11e9-8cb2-799a3a8cf37b.

Fundz. "Series A, B, C Funding: The Ultimate Guide." Accessed May 30, 2020. https://www.fundz.net/what-is-series-a-funding-series-b-funding-and-more.

Gallo, Carmine. "Apple Retail Stores and the 'Buying Brain.'" *Entrepreneur*. April 24, 2012. https://www.entrepreneur.com/article/223406.

Giacobbe, Alyssa. "How Glossier Hacked Social Media to Build A Cult-Like Following." *Entrepreneur*. August 15, 2017. https://www.entrepreneur.com/article/298014.

Glossier. "About." Accessed May 30, 2020. https://www.glossier.com/about.

Glossier. "Referral Program Terms & Conditions." Accessed May 30, 2020. https://www.glossier.com/referral-terms.

Goldman Sachs. "Emily Weiss: Rethinking the Business of Beauty." January 18, 2019. Video, 20:44. https://youtu.be/zSQ0b0Mmqrk.

Huber, Hannah. "The Top 5 Things We Want to Copy from Glossier's New L.A. Store." *Architectural Digest*. June 4, 2018. https://www.architecturaldigest.com/story/design-ideas-glossier-los-angeles-store.

Lammertink, Inge. "Why Glossier Embodies the Future of Shopping and B2C Marketing." *Medium*. February 11, 2019. https://medium.com/swlh/why-glossier-embodies-the-future-of-shopping-and-b2c-marketing-6b88a863ebc5.

Larocca, Amy. "The Magic Skin of Glossier's Emily Weiss." *The Cut*. January 8, 2018. https://www.thecut.com/2018/01/glossier-emily-weiss.html.

Lawson, Richard. "Online Makeup Startup Invites Customers Inside With a 'Stairway to Heaven.'" *LoopNet*. March 26, 2019. https://www.loopnet.com/learn/online-makeup-startup-invites-customers-inside-with-a-stairway-to-heaven/676004211/.

Mandell, Janna. "Glossier Just Got $52 Million In Fresh Capital, Bringing Total Funding To $86 Million." *Forbes*. February 22, 2018. https://www.forbes.com/sites/jannamandell/2018/02/22/glossier-just-got-52-million-in-fresh-capital-bringing-total-funding-to-86-million/#61ee62c612b6.

Meltzer, Marisa. "How Emily Weiss's Glossier Grew From Millennial Catnip to Billion-Dollar Juggernaut." *Vanity Fair*. October 10, 2019. https://www.vanityfair.com/style/2019/10/how-emily-weiss-grew-glossier-from-millennial-catnip-to-billion-dollar-juggernaut.

Mlotek, Haley. "How Glossier Harnessed The Myth Of Cool Girl Makeup." *The Fader*. August 17, 2016. https://www.thefader.com/2016/08/17/glossier-makeup-emily-weiss-interview.

Ohanian, Alexis. "Emily Weiss." *Time*. Accessed May 30, 2020. https://time.com/collection/time-100-next-2019/5718865/emily-weiss/.

Peterson, Hayley. "VSCO Girls Are Upending the Cosmetics Industry by Eschewing Makeup in Favor of Facial Sprays and Creams." *Business Insider*. October 23, 2019. https://www.businessinsider.com/vsco-girls-upend-beauty-industry-not-wearing-makeup-2019-10.

Recode. "Glossier CEO Emily Weiss | Full Interview | 2018 Code Commerce." September 18, 2018. Video, 31:10. https://youtu.be/wf_6gA7ozgI.

Reiff, Nathan. "Series A, B, C Funding: How It Works." Investopedia. March 5, 2020. https://www.investopedia.com/articles/personal-finance/102015/series-b-c-funding-what-it-all-means-and-how-it-works.asp.

Sojit, Camille. "Glossier, #NoMakeup, and the Authenticity Myth." *Document Journal.* November 4, 2019. https://www.document-journal.com/2019/11/glossier-nomakeup-and-the-authenticity-myth/.

Villena, Kayla. "Millennial Beauty." Euromonitor International. January 23, 2019. https://blog.euromonitor.com/millennial-beauty/.

Walton, Chris. "Glossier To Open New Flagship Store In New York." *Forbes.* November 5, 2018. https://www.forbes.com/sites/christopherwalton/2018/11/05/glossier-to-open-new-flagship-store-in-new-york-this-week/#2925cbd5295b.

CHAPTER 11

Anastasia Beverly Hills. "About Anastasia Beverly Hills." Accessed May 30, 2020. https://www.anastasiabeverlyhills.com/about-us.html.

Anastasia Beverly Hills. "A Visual Timeline." Accessed May 30, 2020. https://www.anastasiabeverlyhills.com/the-arch/?bcid=a-visual-timeline.

Beautylish. "The History of Anastasia Beverly Hills." August 4, 2013. Video, 4:20. https://youtu.be/otfmbuhUQA4.

Boren, Lisa. "Soare." *Los Angeles Business Journal.* July 19, 1999. https://labusinessjournal.com/news/1999/jul/19/soare/.

Clement, J. "Instagram: Most-Followed Beauty Brands 2019." Statista. December 3, 2019. https://www.statista.com/statistics/536991/leading-beauty-brands-instagram-followers/.

Erlich, Jessica Prince. "How I Get It Done: Beauty Entrepreneur Anastasia Soare." *The Cut.* January 2, 2018. https://www.thecut.com/2018/01/how-i-get-it-done-eyebrow-entrepreneur-anastasia-soare.html.

Forbes. "Anastasia Soare." June 3, 2019. https://www.forbes.com/profile/anastasia-soare/#7a4815c92fca.

Harper's Bazaar. "Eyebrow Queen Anastasia Soare Shows off Her Insane Beauty Collection." June 28, 2019. Video, 10:43. https://youtu.be/7NdLjldB9c4.

Meisner, Gary. "Phi and the Golden Section in Architecture." The Golden Number. March 5, 2013. https://www.goldennumber.net/architecture/.

Michael, Souzan. "Anastasia Soare (of Anastasia Beverly Hills) Told Us The Secrets to Her Brand's Massive Success." *Fashion Magazine.* October 15, 2018. https://fashionmagazine.com/face-body/anastasia-soare-anastasia-beverly-hills/.

Reeder, Alyssa, and Anastasia Soare. "Anastasia Soare Of Anastasia Beverly Hills Shares Her Beauty Routine." *Into The Gloss.* May 19, 2015. https://intothegloss.com/2015/06/anastasia-soare-founder-anastasia-beverly-hills/.

Schmidt, Ingrid. "Eyebrow Guru Anastasia Soare's 'A-Ha!' Moment? It Was Inspired by Da Vinci. Now, 'She Creates a

Masterpiece.'" *Los Angeles Times.* December 14, 2017. https://www.latimes.com/fashion/la-ig-anastasia-beverly-hills-salon-20171217-story.html.

CHAPTER 12

Abelman, Devon. "Beauty Bakerie Lip Whip Will Not Budge for Anything." *Allure.* November 11, 2016. https://www.allure.com/story/beauty-bakerie-lip-whip-stay-put.

Beauty Bakerie. "Our Story." Accessed May 30, 2020. https://www.beautybakerie.com/pages/about-us.

Beauty Bakerie. "Sugar Homes." Accessed May 30, 2020. https://www.beautybakerie.com/pages/sugar-homes#page-4.

Cacciatore, Bella. "Cashmere Nicole Is What a 2019 CEO Looks Like." *Glamour.* August 13, 2019. https://www.glamour.com/story/cashmere-nicole-woty-all-year.

Crunchbase. "Series A—Beauty Bakerie Cosmetics Brand." July 9, 2018. https://www.crunchbase.com/funding_round/beauty-bakerie-cosmetics-brand-series-a--54d4593f#section-overview.

Digitalundivided. "ProjectDiane2018." Accessed May 30, 2020. http://www.projectdiane.com/.

D'Spain, Ethan. "Beauty Bakerie's Cashmere Nicole Is Better, Not Bitter." *Paper.* December 4, 2018. https://www.papermag.com/beauty-bakerie-cashmere-nicole-2622412620.html?rebelltitem=10#rebelltitem10.

Feldman, Amy. "How A Single Mom Battling Breast Cancer Built Beauty Bakerie To A $5M Brand, Got Unilever To Invest." *Forbes.* December 3, 2017. https://www.forbes.com/sites/amyfeldman/2017/12/03/how-a-single-mom-battling-breast-cancer-built-beauty-bakerie-to-a-5m-brand-got-unilever-to-invest/#250cb94343f8.

Ginzburg, Jean. "'Study, Never Stop Looking for More Information' with Cashmere Nicole." Medium. August 16, 2018. https://medium.com/authority-magazine/study-never-stop-looking-for-more-information-with-cashmere-nicole-43c2e84cceaf.

Jackie Aina. "Full Face of Women-Owned Beauty Brands." November 21, 2017. Video, 21:06. https://youtu.be/taxAD2LePy8.

KathleenLights. "Full Face Beauty Bakerie | First Impressions." August 8, 2018. Video, 18:20. https://youtu.be/YDmDf2HaC7k.

Lawrence, Shammara. "Beauty Bakerie CEO Cashmere Nicole Opens Up About the Inclusive Indie Makeup Brand's Massive Success." *Allure.* May 1, 2018. https://www.allure.com/story/beauty-bakerie-cashmere-nicole-interview-inclusivity-makeup-mission.

Lawrence, Shammara. "The Beauty Brands to Know Helmed by Black Women." Medium, February 17, 2020. https://medium.com/supermaker-com/the-beauty-brands-to-know-helmed-by-black-women-cbdc625d75ea.

Pelletiere, Nicole. "How Beauty Bakerie Founder Cashmere Nicole Went from Food Stamps to Launching a Multi-Million Dollar Cosmetics Brand." *ABC News.* October 8, 2018. https://abcnews.go.com/GMA/Style/beauty-bakerie-founder-cashmere-nicole-food-stamps-launching/story?id=58311180.

Simeon, Aimee. "How Breast Cancer & Beyoncé Fueled This Beauty Mogul's Appetite For Success." *Refinery29.* November 6, 2018. https://www.refinery29.com/en-us/beauty-bakerie-founder-cashmere-nicole-interview.

Tati. "Beauty Bakerie | Hot or Not." June 15, 2017. Video, 13:36. https://youtu.be/O_FOjp5yc5I.

Uwumarogie, Victoria. "Cashmere Nicole Put Off Seeing A Doctor About The Lump In Her Breast Until It Was Too Big Too Ignore—And Cancerous." *MadameNoire.* October 29, 2019. https://madamenoire.com/1110009/cashmere-nicole-breast-cancer/.

Villena, Kayla. "Millennial Beauty." Euromonitor International. January 23, 2019. https://blog.euromonitor.com/millennial-beauty/.

Wischhover, Cheryl. "3 Founders on How to Build a Modern Beauty Brand." *Vogue Business.* June 16, 2019. https://www.voguebusiness.com/beauty/branding-in-beauty-founders-startups.

CHAPTER 13

Bergman, Sirena. "How Jaclyn Hill's Lipstick Scandal Could Transform the YouTube Make-up Industry Forever." *The Independent.* June 14, 2019. https://www.independent.co.uk/life-style/fashion/jaclyn-hill-youtube-lipstick-cosmetics-petition-fda-james-charles-tati-a8958641.html.

Capon, Laura. "Morphe Has Delayed the Launch of Their Jaclyn Hill Vault Collection after Poor YouTube Reviews." *Cosmopolitan.* June 22, 2018. https://www.cosmopolitan.com/uk/beauty-hair/makeup/a21760856/morphe-jaclyn-hill-vault-eyeshadow-palette-bad-reviews-delay-recall/.

Change.org. "Recall Jaclyn Cosmetics." Accessed May 31, 2020. https://www.change.org/p/jaclyn-hill-recall-jaclyn-cosmetics?recruiter=957521647&utm_source=share_petition&utm_medium=twitter&utm_campaign=psf_combo_share_abi&utm_term=psf_combo_share_initial&recruited_by_

id=84aec120-6ed7-11e9-8def-c3242d4de6b0&share_bandit_exp=abi-16042321-en-US&share_bandit_var=v3.

Collins, Allison. "Facetime With Jaclyn Hill, Vlogger and Social Media Influencer." *WWD*. June 29, 2016. https://wwd.com/business-news/human-resources/jaclyn-hill-vlogger-social-media-becca-10475043/.

Diaz, Thatiana. "Jaclyn Hill Is Giving Every Person Who Bought Her Lipstick A Refund." *Refinery29*. June 24, 2019. https://www.refinery29.com/en-us/2019/06/236206/jaclyn-hill-refund-lipstick-controversy-no-recall.

Guglielmetti, Petra. "Everything Jaclyn Hill Touches Sells Out Instantly." *Glamour*. January 5, 2016. https://www.glamour.com/story/jaclyn-hill-makeup-brushes-palette.

Jackie Aina. "Jaclyn Hill x Morphe Vault: They Almost Had Me In the First Half Not Gonna Lie." June 17, 2018. Video, 17:42. https://youtu.be/uVGM7Qz_nOw.

Jaclyn Hill. "Introducing Jaclyn Cosmetics." May 23, 2019. Video, 35:39. https://youtu.be/fPFMPnnwBVQ.

Jaclyn Hill. "Jaclyn Cosmetics Holiday Collection Reveal." November 14, 2019. Video, 32:49. https://youtu.be/2ChGG_FA1Q4.

Jaclyn Hill. "My Lipsticks." June 12, 2019. Video, 14:02. https://youtu.be/x8QeSZprobs.

Jaclyn Hill. "The Jaclyn Hill Palette Volume 2 Reveal + Swatches." February 10, 2020. Video, 33:25. https://youtu.be/JFTAN_NA4wk.

Jaclyn Hill. "Where I've Been." July 23, 2019. Video, 19:02. https://youtu.be/Q7-brNoqCqI.

Krause, Amanda. "A Complete Timeline of Beauty YouTuber Jaclyn Hill's Disastrous Lipstick Launch." *Insider.* June 14, 2019. https://www.insider.com/jaclyn-hill-lipstick-controversy-timeline-2019-6.

RawBeautyKristi. "The Truth About Jaclyn Hill Cosmetics Lipstick." June 8, 2019. Video, 52:16. https://youtu.be/VWedI5Csjhw.

Rearick, Lauren. "Jaclyn Hill Deleted Her Social Media Following the Controversial Release of Her Jaclyn Hill Cosmetics Lipstick Line." *Teen Vogue.* July 3, 2019. https://www.teenvogue.com/story/jaclyn-hill-deleted-social-media-jaclyn-hill-cosmetics-lipstick.

Simmons, Shea. "Are Jaclyn Hill's So Rich Lipsticks Sold Out? Here's What's Left From The First Launch." *Bustle.* May 31, 2019. https://www.bustle.com/p/are-jaclyn-hills-so-rich-lipsticks-sold-out-heres-whats-left-from-the-first-launch-17939194.

Marlena Stell. Twitter post. June 9, 2019. https://twitter.com/MarlenaStell/status/1137806562032930816.

Tea Spill. "Marlena Stell EXPOSES the Beauty Community." June 27, 2019. Video, 11:26. https://youtu.be/BcSXolIUxSM.

Tinubu, Abeni. "Why Jaclyn Hill Fans Are Hesitant To Forgive Her For The Lipstick Drama." Showbiz Cheat Sheet. September 24, 2019. https://www.cheatsheet.com/entertainment/jaclyn-hill-lipstick-drama.html/.

Social Blade. "Jaclyn Hill." Accessed May 31, 2020. https://socialblade.com/youtube/user/jaclynhill1.

CHAPTER 14

Archer, Sarah. "*Tidying Up With Marie Kondo* Isn't Really a Makeover Show." *The Atlantic.* January 4, 2019. https://www.

theatlantic.com/entertainment/archive/2019/01/tidying-up-with-marie-kondo-netflix-show-kon-mari-review/579400/.

Kimberly Clark. "Best of Antihauls!—Helpful Tips, Rants and Reads." September 28, 2017. Video, 33:11. https://youtu.be/ArH_G-u4ojc.

KonMari. "About KonMari." Accessed May 31, 2020. https://shop.konmari.com/pages/about.

Laura Lee. "Huge Anti Haul | Makeup I Will Not Be Buying." October 27, 2019. Video, 24:24. https://youtu.be/U4HscLZxhvU.

Lauren Curtis. "Goodbye PR Packages ... Makeup Cull." November 28, 2018. Video, 8:12. https://youtu.be/mHeHQPX9RIA.

Netflix. "Makeup Mayham." *Broken* Season 1, Episode 1. November 27, 2019. https://www.netflix.com/watch/81002634?trackId=200257859

Peterson, Hayley. "VSCO Girls Are Upending the Cosmetics Industry by Eschewing Makeup in Favor of Facial Sprays and Creams." *Business Insider.* October 23, 2019. https://www.businessinsider.com/vsco-girls-upend-beauty-industry-not-wearing-makeup-2019-10.

RawBeautyKristi. "Makeup I Am Not Going to Buy ... Anti-Haul." October 17, 2019. Video, 31:59. https://youtu.be/xa7XZF4wA7o.

Samantha Ravndahl. "No More PR." November 16, 2018. Video, 24:17. https://youtu.be/oyoblecIPwE.

Samantha Ravndahl. "Three Month No Buy ... How Did That Go." December 31, 2019. Video, 19:25. https://youtu.be/aW6ybgpHDjQ.

Sunmark Publishing. "KonMari Books." Accessed May 31, 2020. http://www.mariekondobooks.com/.

The New York Times. "Advice, How-To & Miscellaneous Books—Best Sellers." January 20, 2018. https://www.nytimes.com/books/best-sellers/2018/01/20/advice-how-to-and-miscellaneous/.

Zeisler, Andi. "Are Anti-Hauls the Antidote to YouTube's Cult of Consumerism." *Bitch Media*. June 18, 2019. https://www.bitchmedia.org/article/antihauls-youtube-consumerism.

Tati. "This Needs to Stop." December 5, 2019. Video, 18:00. https://youtu.be/ovDit1-xArA.

CONCLUSION

Castellanos, Sara. "Estée Lauder Revamps IT, Merging Beauty Business With Innovation." *The Wall Street Journal*. March 20, 2019. https://www.wsj.com/articles/estee-lauder-revamps-it-merging-beauty-business-with-innovation-11553120039.

Encyclopaedia Britannica. s.v. "Minstrel Show." May 19, 2020. https://www.britannica.com/art/minstrel-show.

Garcia, Ahiza. "The Skincare Industry Is Booming, Fueled by Informed Consumers and Social Media." *CNN*. May 10, 2019. https://www.cnn.com/2019/05/10/business/skincare-industry-trends-beauty-social-media/index.html.

Jackson, Lauren Michele. "Shudu Gram Is a White Man's Digital Projection of Real-Life Black Womanhood." *The New Yorker*. May 4, 2018. https://www.newyorker.com/culture/culture-desk/shudu-gram-is-a-white-mans-digital-projection-of-real-life-black-womanhood.

J.P. Morgan. "How Technology Is Giving the Beauty Industry a Makeover." Accessed June 1, 2020. https://www.jpmorgan.com/global/research/beauty-industry.

Peterson, Hayley. "VSCO Girls Are Upending the Cosmetics Industry by Eschewing Makeup in Favor of Facial Sprays and Creams." *Business Insider.* October 23, 2019. https://www.businessinsider.com/vsco-girls-upend-beauty-industry-not-wearing-makeup-2019-10.

Rosenstein, Jenna. "People Can't Tell If This Fenty Model Is Real Or Fake." *Harper's Bazaar.* February 9, 2018. https://www.harpersbazaar.com/beauty/makeup/a16810663/shudu-gram-fenty-model-fake/.

Shudu.gram. Instagram. Accessed June 1, 2020. https://www.instagram.com/shudu.gram/.

Song, Victoria. "Olay Convinced Me to Moisturize By Showing Me What I'll Look Like in 20 Years." Gizmodo. January 9, 2019. https://gizmodo.com/olay-convinced-me-to-moisturize-by-showing-me-what-ill-1831615771.

Tietjen, Alexa. "Influencer Ex Machina." *WWD.* July 11, 2018. https://wwd.com/beauty-industry-news/beauty-features/influencer-ex-machina-shudu-lil-miquela-virtual-celebrities-instagram-1202755789/.

Winter, Dayna. "Powering the Pout: The (Other) Woman Behind Kylie Cosmetics." Shopify. May 11, 2017. https://www.shopify.com/blog/214945353-seed-beauty-kylie-cosmetics.

ACKNOWLEDGEMENTS

I would like to recognize those who have supported me throughout this publishing journey. This book would not have been possible without the insight and encouragement of a community of people who believed in me. Thank you to each of you who helped me turn my childhood dream of being an author into a reality.

First and foremost, I want to acknowledge my family. Thank you to my parents, Costina and Dan, and my grandparents, Gina, Stella, Traian, for encouraging me to love learning. Thank you to my brother, Victor, for being my lifelong friend. Thank you to my partner, Kiarie, for picking me up each time I fell.

Thank you to my interviewees, whose observations about the beauty industry inspired many of my ideas:

Alexandra Morris	Kiarie Mumbi
Ashly Paulino	Leanne Almeida
Daana Bajnauth	Madeline Moreno
Grace Shin	Natalie Wong
Kaie Jarvis	Racquel Jones

Thank you to everybody who contributed to and promoted my publishing campaign. Without you, this book would not have become a reality:

Adam Shlomi	Kolade Lawal
Adina Pacuraru	Laurie Dhue
Adriana and Adrian Voicu	Leanne Almeida
Alexandra Morris	Madeline Moreno
Anna Beloborodova	Maria Gabriela Solotchi
Anthony Obas	Maria Somoza
Ashly Paulino	Mariana Batsu
Bianca Cioclei	Mihaela McCallum
Christopher Mungiello	Monica Raicea
Daniel King	Myiah Smith
Daniela Datcu	Natalie Wong
Doris Capet	Nicole Shipe-Olivares
Eric Koester	Nonni Rita
Ethan Ramer	Octavia Catana
Helen Su	Patricia Lee-Hruska
Helene Abou-Rjaili (Special Recognition)	Pramiksha Marcharchand
	Racquel Jones
Isha Battu	Ralph Russo
Jasmine Shaw	Sho Nosaka
Jianhua Tian	Shrayus Sortur
Joshua Bae	Sohum Shah
Kaie Jarvis	Tamika Gray
Kiarie Mumbi	

Thank you to Professor Eric Koester for setting me on this path and having faith in my abilities from the very beginning. Thank you to Jemiscoe Chambers-Black, my editor, for helping me discover and refine my author's voice. Thank you to *New Degree Press* for embracing my vision.

I would also like to recognize everybody else who is not mentioned in this Acknowledgements section and who helped me get to this point in my life.

www.ingramcontent.com/pod-product-compliance
Lightning Source LLC
LaVergne TN
LVHW011815060526
838200LV00053B/3789